T0407473

THE SPINNER'S
BLENDING BOARD
BIBLE

From Woolen to (Nearly!) Worsted and Everything in Between

DEBORAH HELD

STACKPOLE BOOKS

Essex, Connecticut
Blue Ridge Summit, Pennsylvania

STACKPOLE BOOKS

An imprint of the Globe Pequot Publishing Group, Inc.
64 South Main Street
Essex, CT 06426
GlobePequot.com

Copyright © 2025 Deborah Held
Photography by Deborah Held

British Library Cataloguing in Publication Information available

Library of Congress Cataloging-in-Publication Data available

ISBN 978-0-8117-7367-6 (cloth : alk. paper)
ISBN 978-0-8117-7368-3 (electronic)

♻️™ The paper used in this publication meets the minimum requirements of American National Standard for Information Sciences—Permanence of Paper for Printed Library Materials, ANSI/NISO Z39.48-1992.

First Edition

To my mom, Lois Held, the strongest, most positive person I know, and my dad, Kalman Held, of blessed memory, whose bright light helped illuminate my way in this world for more than five decades.

You are forever missed.

CONTENTS

3: ROLLED-OFF PREPARATIONS: ROLAGS, ROLLED LOGS, PUNIS, AND ROLY-POLIES 41

FOREWORD

This is an exciting moment for you. You're about to turn the pages and enter into a brilliant, colorful world of fiber preparation with one of the most enthusiastic and encouraging spinning educators I know—Debbie Held.

Years ago, Debbie and I became acquainted over our shared love of spinning and fiber. Debbie had a kind of playful and positive energy that helped me feel more free and at ease with experimenting and trying new things with my spinning. In my personal journey of learning to spin, I gripped tightly to the belief that to be a really good and accomplished spinner, I needed to do all the right things and spin in a disciplined way to create "perfect" yarn. I felt compelled to scale the challenge of spinning as thin and as fine as I could, to somehow prove my spinning ability. And I always felt the overarching need to perfect my skills so that I could create a handspun yarn that rivalled mill-spun yarn. But the more I spun in this way, the less fun I had. I was always self-critical of what I had spun, no matter how it turned out. It could always be better; I could have always done better.

After Debbie and I connected over those first messages, I've since had the chance to have great, deeper conversations with her about spinning and the fiber arts. Debbie has joined us at the School of SweetGeorgia to teach new and experienced spinners alike about fiber, fiber prep, and spinning. I've learned so much from watching and listening to her teach, and her whole perspective on spinning has transformed my personal feeling and experience of spinning, too.

I'm so much more relaxed with my spinning now. I'm so much more open to just having fun with it. There is absolutely something to be said about practicing your skills and techniques, learning the different drafting and plying methods and how they could be employed, but there is also something to be said about just letting go and playing with your materials.

I think about watching my young kids playing with clay or slime, and how the joy is in the sensory play. Just seeing colors mix and combine. Feeling the texture of the materials flow through your fingers and your tools. Seeing colors transformed through the act of blending, breaking up, and optically remixing hues. All of this is magical and beautiful.

Debbie's book is a delight, because in these pages she shares her deep love of fiber preparation with a humble, accessible, and unassuming tool—a blending board. I love how Debbie demonstrates how a simple DIY blending board can provide just as much blending capability as a more expensive piece of fiber prep equipment.

With a blending board, Debbie shows us an incredible number of ways to play with different colors, textures, and fibers to create everything from rolags to punis to batts, and so much more.

As I read through Debbie's instructions, I got that creative itch to grab my blending board, pull out my spinning fiber stash, and just *play*. The photographs will spark inspiration and your imagination. You'll soon discover that with blending boards, the possibilities are endless. Whether you love spinning woolen yarns from rolags or smooth worsted yarns from near perfectly aligned top, the blending board can create all these fiber preparations. Debbie shows us that one tool can rule them all!

This book is perfect for spinners who love the tactile, sensory joy of playing with fiber and learning fiber preparation techniques. Perhaps you'll discover that you enjoy the preparation process even more than spinning itself!

—Felicia Lo, Founder & Creative Director, SweetGeorgia Yarns

INTRODUCTION

As spinning tools go, the modern blending board as we know it is relatively new. So, while there's a whole lot of interest in learning to use it, there's still not much in the way of deep, informational education on the topic. I wanted to change that by writing an in-depth reference book on the blending board and how to maximize its potential, as I believe it to be a woefully undervalued, yet powerful tool for fiber preparation. Better still, the simple build allows us to utilize the blending board across the woolen to (nearly) worsted fiber prep spectrum, almost endlessly.

I got my first blending board very early in my spinning journey when, like many, I caught the urge to play with color placement, texture, and basic fiber preparation in my spinning. I knew very little about, well . . . anything, and my choices in fiber and the yarns I wanted to spin from it were mostly based on my favorite colors and a love of smooth, fluffy batts. I knew almost nothing about fiber traits such as crimp, elasticity, hardiness, etc., at the time, and certainly had no in-depth classical spinning knowledge.

I chose a blending board over hand cards or combs, as money was so tight for me that I bartered my writing services for not just this blending board but also my first spinning wheel. (A drum carder was entirely out of the question for me financially, so I put that wish off on the horizon.) I'd intended for this blending board to be my introductory, "for now" carding tool. I liked it from the start as it was easy to store in my small apartment and it was fun to use. I made rolags and airy batts, and initially, I was content with that.

As I learned more about classical spinning techniques and eventually merged my career in business writing with my love of handspinning and the desire to write about it, I knew that I needed to put my blending board to use even more effectively. Indeed, my very first spinning-related article was on best practices for using a blending board (thank you, Anne Merrow, then editor of *Spin Off* magazine),[1] for which I interviewed Beth Lower of the former Blue Mountain Handcrafts, Jessica Henderson of the former Topeka Twister, and April Wolf of Phoenix Fiber Company, also now shuttered. Each of these women ran fiber and dyeing businesses for years where their blending boards

---

1 *Spin Off*, 2016, "Blending Board Tips."

served as their primary or main blending tool, and they all generously shared their tips and tricks with me. I was hooked.

In the years since, my blending board has served me well. To this day, it remains my most-used fiber processing tool. Yes, I finally landed that drum carder many years later, but by then I was so adept at making my blending board work to meet my every preparatory need that even I couldn't distinguish the items I created on it from those made on my drum carder.[2] The more years I spend using my blending board and growing as a spinner, the more usage ideas it still sparks. It is my go-to for creating everything from (the obvious) rolags, to gloriously fluffy batts and lightly tweedy rovings, clouds, and more. I am able to prepare every conceivable color-blending and textural result I can imagine: stripes, tweedy pops, heathers, gradients galore, fractals, etc.

As a fiber arts educator, I love the excitement on my students' faces as the potential uses for the blending board are unlocked, such as the time when a group of students in Scotland ran up to their hotel rooms to gather their hairbrushes when there weren't enough "real" blending brushes for everyone to use at once. They were so pleased with the blending results that even those who were working with the true blending brushes ran for their hairbrushes, too.

My spinning mission is to help as many spinners as possible to recognize the potential of this humble, affordable, space-efficient blending and carding tool. I hope this book helps you see your own blending board in a whole new way!

---

2 *Ply Magazine*, Mix Issue 2022, "Prep it! Blending Board Beauty."

1

YOUR BLENDING BOARD: THE ALL-IN-ONE FIBER-PROCESSING TOOL

Modern handspinners don't spin yarn because we need to; we spin our own yarn because we love to—and because we can. We no longer need these handspun threads to make our clothes and keep our families warm, nor must we spend countless hours running our homes and homesteads by day and hand-processing pounds of fiber for spinning by night. Today we have the luxury of taking joy from our basic connection to this ancient craft and the meditative qualities each step of the process can provide. And while hand-preparing fiber and deciding which spinning tools to purchase first and in what order may feel overwhelming initially, there's an all-in-one tool for fiber preparation that's been overlooked for far too long. That tool is the unassuming but powerfully adaptive blending board.

Hand-processing tools are costly, and each has its own best purpose, be it for hand-carding short, fine fibers or combing a longer-stapled wool destined for a crisp-knitted outerwear cable. There's a place for all such equipment in the cache of a dedicated spinner, but identifying the spinner you will become takes years, and one's path may wind . . . as it should! Further, we each have our own unique limitations, be they physical, spatial, or financial—or even all of these and more.

That's why I confidently recommend a blending board and an open mind to any spinner who's looking to play with fiber and color blending and, of course, with woolen to worsted-style fiber preparation. With a focused approach, the blending board is truly an all-in-one processing tool that does no one singular thing and yet everything, thanks to its large, flat surface space and deceptively simple engineering. You can use a blending board to bring a compacted braid of fiber back to life, blend one-of-a-kind or repeatable colorways (in a single pass or multiple passes), and card cloud-light rolags and denser punis. You can utilize the teeth of your blending board to closely replicate a combed top and pull or diz a roving using any number of methods. If you're interested in fleece, your blending board can even serve as a tool for flick-carding locks and lining them up for seamless spinning, and for carding up a woolen cloud. It's ideal for blending colors, planning and executing color repeats, and carding textures that whisper or sing. You can prepare fibers and blends for fractal-style spinning, strong worsted-like spinning, and lofty woolen spinning; and, if your interests veer toward artful wet felting . . . the blending board is ideally suited for that process, too.

Your blending board is easily stored away when not in use, no matter how small your living space. It's transportable, too. Using and getting to know your blending board can help you unlock the creativity within and become a better spinner, with a greater understanding of your craft and other yarn-related hobbies.

BREAKING DOWN THE BLENDING BOARD

History and Manufacturing

The handspinning community has fiber equipment company Clemes & Clemes and spinner Gwen Powell to thank for bringing us the modern-day blending board. It was sometime around 2010 when Powell approached the company to collaborate and develop an alternative means for those interested in carding quantities of rolags for woolen spinning without the expense and physical strain of using a drum carder. The immediate interest was so great that other big-name spinning tool manufacturers and smaller makers entered the market with their own blending boards almost immediately, and the appeal remains equally strong to this day. What *has* changed in these years—at least on the part of some makers—is the carding cloth used and the innumerable ways we spinners have learned to maximize the blending board's utility.

Today, the design itself remains universally similar from outward appearances: a good-sized carding cloth (typically around 12 in. x 12 in. [30.5 x 30.5 cm]) that's secured to a flat wood surface of similar or larger size. Different makers and brands may put more or less focus on aesthetics like wood type and finishing, but all commercial blending boards share these main features, plus other subtle, simple design elements like a detachable swivel keel to aid in an ergonomic experience.

Commercially made blending boards almost always have a detachable swivel keel,[3] some with multiple angles to choose from. The knob and swivel keel, among other uses, allow the user to load the board and card fiber at a comfortable 45

3   According to Roy and Henry Clemes, Gwen, a lover of sailboat racing, suggested the name "keel" for this support piece as it reminded her of the support keel used beneath a vessel along the centerline of its hull.

Figure 1.1 Left, Ashford blending board; right, Brother Drum Carder blending board.

Figure 1.2 Blending board by Majacraft.

Figure 1.3 The keel can be set vertically or horizontally, per the user's preference to sit or stand. When vertical, the keel may be held between the seated user's legs. From this position, the surface of the board may also be swiveled 45 degrees to either side for an ergonomic carding experience. It's also designed to swivel the board fully upside down, which may be more comfortable for some when rolling off prepared fibers.

degrees to their left or right to combat shoulder strain. When set horizontally (figure 1.3), the keel helps the user work at a comfortable angle and height for their preferences. The keel may also be swiveled so it's aligned vertically to the board where it can sit between the user's legs for stability, both when working on and rolling off the prepared fibers. By keeping the keel slightly loosened, the seated user can swivel the board to their left or right, for a shoulder-friendly, 45-degree (or so) loading and carding angle.

Further, the keel can also be used to secure the blending board to the lip of the desk or table you're working on to help tension your roll-offs and to keep the board in place while blending (figure 1.4).

Figure 1.4 When the keel is screwed into the lowest angle (closest to the handle) of the board and in the horizontal position, it may be used to secure and tension the board against the lip of a table for security in carding and well-tensioned roll-offs.

Figure 1.5 "Knee" curves on one end make it easy to invert your blending board.

Figure 1.6 Belly grooves and cutout thumb tensioning divots were added by this now-shuttered maker, for optimal comfort.

Any blending board with a keel may be swiveled anywhere from fully right-side up to all the way upside down, as some users find that the fiber releases from the carding teeth more easily from this direction. This is also the ergonomic reason for the symmetrical cutout "knee" curves sometimes seen on the top sides of many blending boards (figure 1.5). While they're not a necessity, these grooves make turning your blending board upside down more comfortable.

The maker of my very first blending board—a company that is no longer in business—designed and cut a thoughtfully inverted, belly-sized curve into the top and bottom of the board's surface, in place of knee grooves (figure 1.6). These "belly holders" provide physical support to the user while working with the blending board, whether it's upright or reversed. This same maker also bore thumb indents into the wood framing both sides of the carding cloth, to aid in tensioning when rolling rolags.

Commercially made blending boards typically have some kind of handle cut into the wood itself or added with hardware. This makes space-saving storage that much easier, as the flat boards can be hung from the wall when not in use and until needed, and transporting the blending board is that much easier too, since it breaks down flat. It should be noted that many users prefer to use their boards flat, or keel-less. A strong clamp or two may be used to hold the board in place when used flat on a table, though a square of rubber, foam, or felt may be used underneath it for the same purpose. It's a matter of personal preference and neither way is right nor wrong.

What's more important to highlight than these overall similarities are the differences in blending boards. They're subtle but impactful. Aesthetic

Figure 1.7 The carrying/hanging handles are cut into the board's surface or added with hardware.

Figure 1.8 U-shaped wire pins are inserted from the underside of any foundation cloth. This shape helps keep the pins from loosening and coming out.

U-shape

differences, such as hand-finished hardwoods vs. unfinished, less expensive softer woods like plywood or oak, and even pressed board, do affect appearance but usually have no bearing on your carding. These are markers for cost and an expression of personal taste and craftsmanship—which may or may not matter to you. At the time of this writing, a wood (pressed or solid) blending board, along with its standard accessories, runs the gamut of $120 to upward of $400,[4] depending mostly on the quality of the wood and woodworking involved and the accessories included, if any. Most hover in the $150 to $225 range. The typical blending board package comes with the board itself, its keel, and some manner of brush—though the included brush may or may not be worth much in terms of true carding abilities. It will also include a pair of dowels for rolling off your prepared fiber. (See chapter 2 regarding inexpensive but all-important additions you can add to your blending board to broaden your fiber prep possibilities.) Again, appearance is a matter of taste and budget. The material that impacts your blending board's performance most of all, aside from aftermarket tools and your own technique, is its carding cloth.

---

4 At the highest cost end is the Clemes & Clemes blending board, which is handmade from a range of hardwoods and utilizes a custom, proprietary blending cloth.

The Truth about Carding Cloth vs. Blending Cloth

This is where the real differences lie. All carding cloth, whether on hand cards, a flicker brush, around a drum, etc., is made of groupings of staple-shaped wires that are inserted in various repeated patterns and rows through the underside of a flexible backing base, or the cloth.

That foundation is made up of canvas and other materials (PVC, leather, felt, rubber, etc.) in a range of layering order and thicknesses, depending on the tool it's meant to cover and its manufacturer or based on custom specifications. Carding cloth has been used for centuries in the textiles industry and in other industries, too, thanks to the advent of specialized commercial machinery during the Industrial Revolution.

There are two types of industrially made carding cloth, known as fillet and sheet. Fillet-style card cloth is made in continuous, narrow rolls. The points of the teeth can be mechanically sharpened for better grip and use in specialty carding. The appropriate length is cut from the roll, ready to be used for its intended application. Wire fillet is the gold standard for drums/cylinders and even machine carding equipment. Sheet-type card cloth is manufactured in sheets, ready to be applied directly to items like the blending board, hand cards, and flicker brushes.

Industrial garneting was introduced during the mechanical boom of the Industrial Revolution to address the need for large-scale salvaging and reuse of yarn and fabric waste. Its job was to shred such waste, returning it to a fibrous, spinnable form to be respun alone or carded with other spinning fiber. Thus, the impetus for the modern blending board—sometimes called a "garneting board" by early adopters—was to allow the home spinner to make the most of sustainable scraps and even design their own yarns using garneted materials.

To the naked and inexperienced eye, fiber arts carding cloth all looks basically the same: a pliable, rubber-topped, layered cloth base with wire teeth (aka tines, pins, etc.). We commonly see this cloth manufactured and offered with differing tine densities, or teeth per square inch (TPI), marketed for coarse, medium, and fine carding. The denser the packing of these tines, the higher the TPI number and the smoother the carding result will be in a single blending pass. "Standard" or moderate TPI is approximately 72 teeth per inch, and universally, TPI numbers range from a coarse 54[5] TPI to a fine 120 TPI, although some manufacturers make an even denser TPI cloth marketed for use with the finest, most luxurious fibers. But carding cloth is a highly specialized business that goes far deeper than mere teeth per inch.

The teeth on any carding cloth serve more than one function. They help to catch and straighten your strands of fiber so that a) the lengthened strands remain in place while they're burnished open and separated with the help of your blending or carding brush, and b) the burnished fiber is smoothed and somewhat distributed across and into the carding surface. Concurrently, the fiber and any added materials blend together. All fiber arts carding cloths have teeth with directional knees, or bends, which help them flex while in use, absorbing the impact of carding while holding onto the fibers. This flexing also helps to protect both the fibers and your equipment from damage. The degree of flex needed varies with the type of equipment and carding cloth used. The smaller licker-in drum on a drum carder, for example, often has shorter, heavier-gauged and stronger tines than those used around the drum carder's main cylinder(s). This allows the licker-in drum to keep the fibers extended until the strands reach the larger, main drum for carding, so they don't snap back

---

5   The numbers are approximate, as density per inch may be impacted by other elements associated with making the filleting or sheet cloth.

Figure 1.9 Teeth placement varies in density, arrangement, and placement on carding cloths of differing TPIs and makers. The pins on the left are grouped in twos with offset rows. The pins on the right side are offset singularly. Both cloths have approximately 72 TPI.

Figure 1.10 Illustration of back view of carding cloth showing a variety of teeth offsets.

on themselves, causing breakage and associated neps. Factors that impact carding teeth flexibility include the type of steel used and its gauge, the location (or pitch) of the knee along the length of the wire and its degree of angle, the length of the wires themselves, their patterning in placement, and even the angle shape and sharpness of their tips (ground or blunted). The materials chosen to make up the backing cloth and their order of layering will also impact the amount of tooth flex possible, as will the materials and method used to affix the cloth to the equipment's surface. (*Glue and other adhesives should never be used underneath a backing cloth, as the pins may settle into the adhesive, negatively impacting their pliability.*) (See appendix A for DIY blending board instructions.)

The past decade-plus since the introduction of the modern blending board has afforded makers and manufacturers time to improve upon the nuances of carding cloths, with some designing cloth that's blending-board specific. Depending on the manufacturer, this cloth typically has slightly longer and finer teeth, allowing for deeper carding and blending, and more flex during the carding process, and it may have a blunted tip for added safety. However, just because a maker or seller uses the term "blending cloth" in their marketing description, doesn't always make it so. There are just a handful of long-standing carding cloth manufacturers and distributors left globally, in locations including the United States, Germany, Belgium, the Netherlands, and Italy. These manufacturers have the knowledge and the dedicated industrial equipment needed to produce carding cloth to a maker's specifications, though sourcing remains challenging as of the writing of this book due to high demand. There are also mass producers of wire fillet in India and China.

In the United States, Howard Brush has been sourcing and creating carding cloth for textiles (and other industries that use wire fillet) since 1866, and they wholesale their standard 54–120 TPI cloths to a major number of blending-board makers and to makers of other hand-carding tools all over the world, including some of the best-known brands.[6] Howard Brush also manufactures carding cloth to custom specification as requested. The company sells a proprietary, true blending cloth for use with the blending board, specifically. The combination of wire length, gauge, bluntness and angle of the tips, pattern placement, and even the materials used in and their order of layering on the foundation cloth itself, were tested for optimal performance and user safety. The company will not confirm the TPI of the cloth, other than to say that it's "around 72 TPI." The placement of the tines is more open than on their standard carding cloth of similar TPI used for drum carding and/or hand carding, which affords the user the option of carding a whole range of fibers and breeds into both smooth and moderately textured batts, rolags, etc., all with the same card cloth. The finer teeth allow for deeper blending and flex while in use and thus less damage to the fibers. The company wholesales this blending cloth to other blending-board makers who then sell it under their own brand names and to some retail suppliers of DIY blending-board materials. It's also sold directly to consumers. Howard Brush uses this same cloth with their own budget-brand blending-board equipment company, Daisy Fiber.

So, is blending cloth different from carding cloth? It depends on the manufacturer, but it certainly can be. *All blending cloth is still carding cloth, and all carding cloth blends fiber*—some are just more effective and efficient than others. Both have the same function, but what we now call "blending" cloth was developed for better and safer use on the flat surface of a blending board.

There are other, quite skilled makers of spinning and fiber prep equipment who have also developed their own specialty blending board–specific card cloths through their own relationships with card cloth manufacturers. This cloth may come from Howard Drum, or it may come from one of the other few remaining manufacturers around the globe. Realistically, it wasn't possible to acquire and try them all for the writing of this book. Rather, my purpose is to educate users so they may select their own best options and get the most from their purchase, no matter the manufacturer. While I do enjoy the true blending cloth myself for its general "do-it-all" potential, I assure you that reading and applying the information in the following chapters will help you get the most out of your blending board, whether it's topped with specialty blending board cloth or a more traditional carding cloth. I spent many years happily using the super-coarse (48 TPI) carding cloth on my first blending board before delving into the writing and researching of this book, and I was thrilled with the results and still use it today.

This is not to say that all carding cloth of the same TPI count performs in exactly the same way. If it's made by the same manufacturer then it will, but sellers don't readily disclose this specific information. Every change (e.g., length and/or gauge of the wire teeth, their pattern placement or grouping, their degree of pitch) influences that equipment's responses to carding in some way.

---

6   For privacy's sake, the company cannot name its customers.

Figure 1.11 These chunky batts were made on my first, 48 TPI, blending board, from a combination of coarse fleece and silken alpaca, plus firestar, silks, Cotswold locks, and Angelina.

The "same" rolags made on two different makers' blending boards may look or feel different, even when those blending boards have the same TPI. *One is not necessarily better than the other, so long as you're able to adjust your own approach to achieve the result you seek.* One of my favorite examples is the Majacraft blending board vs. other blending boards with similar TPI density. Given the same amount of fiber, same carding technique, and using the same dowels and method for roll-off, my rolags trap more air between the individual fibers when I use my Majacraft blending board than with a comparable US-made carding or blending cloth, yielding a loftier result. (Note: This effect is not generated by the visibly narrower surface space of the Majacraft board.)

Using your blending board is like every other aspect of handspinning: Each variable in your approach will have an influence on the resulting yarn. While carding cloth appears straightforward, its materials, manufacturing, and application are all elements in its overall performance. Even the most subtle differences will have some impact on your fiber preparation.

Figures 1.12 and 1.13 Rolags made and rolled from the Majacraft blending board (top two in both photos) vs. those made and rolled from the Brother blending board (bottom two in both photos). Both makers use card cloth with approximately 72 TPI, from different carding cloth manufacturers. The Majacraft card cloth yields an airier roll-off result, despite all other factors remaining the same. Note how the two Majacraft rolags have a fuzzier appearance than those rolled from the Brother board. They also expanded in girth after a few moments off the board, while the Brother rolags expanded/grew lengthwise and have a smoother exterior.

Does TPI Really Matter?

Some blending-board makers offer options of coarse (54) to average (72–90) to fine (96–120) and finest (190) TPI density to their customers, in the same way that makers of drum and hand carders do. Other companies and makers are dedicated to a single TPI option, which usually lands in the average count. The general claim in the fiber community is: The coarser, more open the cloth, the better suited it is to coarser fiber and/or textural elements, and the chunkier and less blended results will be from a single carding pass. This is because a) the pins are firmer and stronger, and

thus have less flex, than those used on cloth with finer TPIs, and b) there is more space between the wire patterning, allowing for broader use in placing textural elements like locks, recycled materials, silk noil, and other such inclusions. The theory works the same in blending colors. Finer TPI is marketed to spinners who work with fine wools and luxury fibers and want a smoother blend of color or materials without the need for multiple carding passes. "In-between" carding cloth is said to perform best with your medium wools and/or slightly textured carding and finer wools that aren't too soft and, therefore, fragile. However, after much testing over several years, I'm going to disagree . . . somewhat. Again, it's all about the performance of the carding cloth combined with the user's technique and the aftermarket tools they use. Yes, a fine carding cloth is ideal for fully and smoothly blending uniquely slick, fine, luxury fibers, and the tines of a coarse cloth make some of the loftiest blends and batts you'll ever see—but it will do so with nearly any fiber combination you can dream up and the proper application and approach. Knowing your goals can be helpful prior to purchasing your blending board or carding cloth, but most of us just don't know these things for certain without experience. The safest bet is the 72 TPI for beginning your journey, unless you know for certain that you'll be focusing on a highly specific superfine or luxury fiber (yak, bison, llama, alpaca and other camelids, etc.) or specifically coarse fiber (Lincoln, Romney, and the like) and textured art batt preparation.

Personally, I suggest erring on the side of a slightly more open cloth than you think you may need, as this will afford you greater flexibility in your fiber preparation now and down the road. A blending board–specific cloth is ideal in all regards, but overall, *you'll be able to achieve practically any result you'd like by putting this book to use with whatever carding cloth and blending board you have or can afford.*

Ultimately, TPI does affect carding results to some degree, though the approachability of the blending board and its aftermarket tools provide the user with more control over outcome than with other carding equipment. So, don't stress too much about which carding (or blending) cloth or maker you choose initially. You can easily and affordably add to your blending tools library by making your own blending board with a different TPI and/or type of cloth. (See appendix A for DIY directions.)

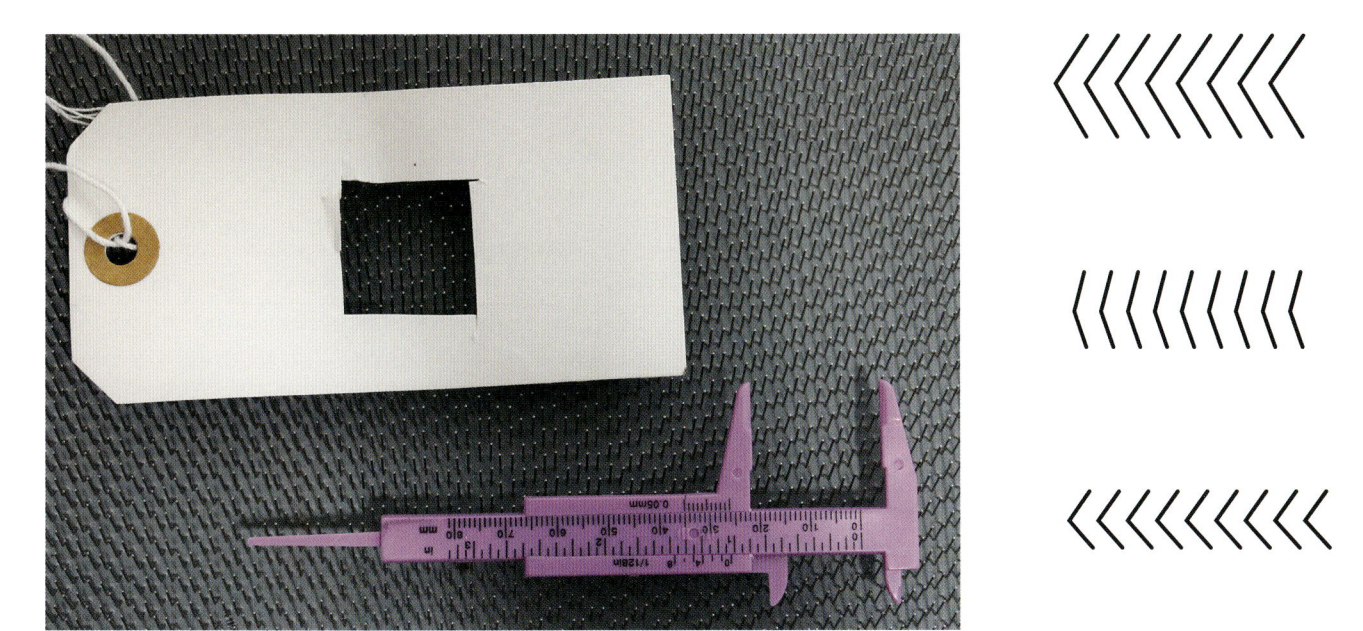

Figure 1.14 Curious about the TPI of your blending or carding cloth? You can decipher the approximate teeth per inch by making a 1 in. by 1 in. square template from strong paper or cardstock. Hold it to your cloth and count the tines in the square. A squared angle tool, such as the one seen here for counting stitches per square inch in knitting swatches, may be used the same way.

Figure 1.15 Tines can vary in pitch angle and placement.

How It Works

As with any carding tools, the act of carding your fiber is dependent on the direction of the teeth themselves. When using a blending board, the knee, or the back side, of the tines should face downward as you work, which means the point portion (figure 1.16) of the tines is facing upward.[7] During carding, these points catch and latch onto the fiber strands to hold them extended as the wire knees flex, protecting the fiber from damage in the process, just as when using a pair of hand cards or a drum carder. What's different (among other things) is the degree of flex and the user's control. A denser TPI will have more flexible tines than a coarser one. It may be helpful to think of your blending board as a giant carding paddle and your choice of blending brush as the top carding paddle (figure 1.17); only here, there's no need to choose a matching set! You can use any TPI brush with any TPI blending board, which is one reason why the blending board is so versatile. In many ways it can function like a drum carder. That top carder or brush acts like the small licker-in drum, which often has a different card cloth and tine structure than the main drum or drums, suited specifically for its job of holding the fiber strands extended as they feed onto the main drum safely, without snap-back damage and associated neps.

Blending board brushes are available online and from sellers of spinning equipment for as little as $20, and all the pertinent traits of carding cloth and wire fillet apply to them, too. When a blending brush is used upside down (held with the knee bends directionally opposite the card cloth below) it will clean your fibers off the board instead of engaging carding, so make sure you know which way is which before you begin burnishing. Similarly, if you're having trouble with a blending brush, try holding it at a different angle when you use it. *Be careful when trying out any carding*

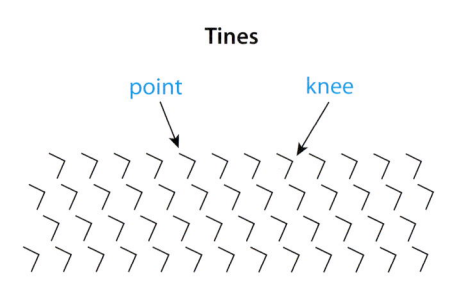

Tines

point   knee

Figure 1.16 The knees of the tines on your blending board should face downward as you work and the points of the tines should be upward.

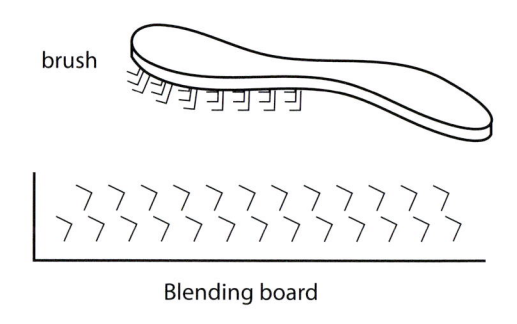

brush

Blending board

Figure 1.17 To card, your brush should be held so its points are also facing upward with its knee bends downward, brushing from the points of the tines toward the knees. (There will be exceptions to this with extra-fine/dense and extra-flexible wire.)

brush against your blending board, no matter the direction of its knees and points. Some are simply too rigid—the tines may be too short or too stiff, or both—and can damage the teeth on the board and/or the cloth backing. This is often the case with brushes that are made for use with a drum carder and with doffing brushes, and even some flick carders with firmer pins that are advertised for use with the blending board. I avoid using any wire-pinned carding brush that's best used with a drum carder. Finer TPI carding cloth or blending-cloth–specific brushes are best for your blending board. The teeth are typically longer and

---

7   This is why you may hear the tines on a card cloth counted in points per square inch, or PPI, instead of tines per square inch, or TPI.

made with fine wire and are thus more pliable, so they can reach all the way down to the top layer of the board's backing cloth and blend without causing damage. In fact, the carding brush's knee—if any—and its direction become less important with increasing fineness of pin gauge and flexibility, but *be advised that these densely packed, (often) kneeless long wires are incredibly sharp*!

When shopping online, you are likely to see slim brushes with moderately stiff nylon bristles labeled as "packing brushes," though they may also be labeled misleadingly as "blending board brushes" for the sake of search engine optimization (SEO) or even by misinformed sellers. These packing brushes do just that—tamp down and pack fiber so you can fit more onto the carding surface and place your fibers and mix-ins or add-ins where you'd like. They don't open the fibers in any notable way. I liken this brush to the attachable

smoothing brush often sold alongside drum carders, only these are manual and appropriately sized for hand use. The bristles are too soft to card open the outer follicles of your fiber, but they're good for placing locks and other dimensional elements without changing the lock structure. They are as effective as your basic household paintbrush but more expensive (and better looking). A tamping brush or a household paintbrush may be included along with your blending-board kit. Unfortunately, an unaware user would be disappointed with their lackluster blending results and might believe that the fault is with their blending board. Still, these tamping brushes are an excellent addition to your cache of carding brushes, which is discussed more thoroughly in chapter 2, along with equally useful brushes you may already have at home or can acquire inexpensively.

Figure 1.18 Fine-wire, kneeless blending brushes are some of the most effective brushes you can use with your blending board, as are fine-toothed blending brushes made with flexible carding cloth. A dense, strong-bristled smoothing brush has its own unique impact and is worth owning, too. Left to right: Fine-wire brushes from Howard Brush and Brother Drum Carder, Strauch's smoothing brush, and a generic pet slicker.

Figure 1.19 Ashford flicker/blending brush (left) and Howard Brush bent-knee blending brush (right).

In sum, the blending board is made all the more versatile with the addition and selection of carding brushes, and they can help you lean into either a more woolen-esque fuzzing and aeration of your fibers or a smoother, more aligned fiber preparation.

Figure 1.20 This beautiful tamping brush (right) is handmade by CF Merchantile, aka Celestial Farms. It's useful for packing fiber into the card cloth, in between the tines. A thick household paintbrush (left) works similarly but is not nearly as pretty.

A COMPARISON OF TOOLS USED IN FIBER PREPARATION

Specialty tools used in fiber preparation are generally thought of as best suited for either carding or combing fiber, though there can be some overlap. Deciding on your first blending tools for fiber processing can be overwhelming, and not everyone can afford the investment. At the time of this writing, a new pair of full-sized hand cards averages about $100; small hand combs cost around the same but can veer into several hundred dollars with more degree of specialty; a blending board ranges from $120 to the mid-$400s; and a drum carder varies between approximately $500 and well into the thousands. Each has its place and its limitations.

Carding

Carding uses wire-tined, flexible specialty cloth to separate, fluff, and redistribute fibers so they spin easily. This preparation is uniquely soft, lofty, and airy. The carding cloth may be on large industrial machinery, home-sized drums, or hand-held equipment. Carding can also draw the fiber grain into something of an alignment, thanks to the wire teeth. This preparation allows the spinner to trap as much air as possible in between the strands and layers of the fiber while spinning, creating a light, woolly, warm yarn—albeit one that is softer in structure and more abradable than a yarn spun from a combed preparation. Carding works especially well with fleece or commercially processed wool top with a short to medium staple length of approximately 1 to 3 inches and with an endless array of inclusions. Carded fiber can run the gamut from looking and feeling silky smooth to highly textured, depending on the carding surface and materials used. Rolags, batts, punis, and roving are all carded preparations.

Each tool has its own best application, but all are adaptable. Many spinners yearn for the Holy Grail of fiber prep, the drum carder, because they believe it offers faster, better results for less energy expended. The truth is, though, putting any of these tools to proper use is time consuming.

Figure 1.21 Equipment for at-home carding includes hand cards, the drum carder, and the blending board.

Combing

Combed fiber yields the exact opposite effect on your fiber and your finished yarn, resulting in a worsted or worsted-like spinning fiber that's smoother, pulled into alignment, and more compressed than carded fiber. The one similarity that combing and carding share is that both help to separate the individual strands of fiber, so they slide past each other freely and make spinning easier. Hand combs and hackles are dedicated combing tools. Combing removes any shorter bits, or second cuts, of fiber and some vegetable matter (aka VM, found in fleece), while aligning the staple direction at the same time. Combed fiber is smooth. It spins into a denser, more worsted yarn, than fiber prepared by carding. This yarn is stronger and tends to be more lustrous than carded fiber, since combing is generally the method of choice for preparing fibers that are longer-stapled—more than 3 inches in length—though this is not a hard-and-fast rule. Hand combs and the hackle may be used to blend fibers and colors together too, though you'll want to stick to smooth materials since textural and shorter elements are combed out in the process, leaving strands that are the same length for spinning. Adding a diz to the hand-combing process pulls the fibers fully into alignment, creating a true combed top and a fully worsted preparation.

Dedicated combing tools come in a variety of pitches (the number of rows) and pin-density distributions. Avid fleece combers will invest in at least a few sets of hand combs, which may cost anywhere from $100 up to several hundred dollars per pair. The hackle is like a stationary, wider comb without a handle. It's clamped to a desk or table where fiber is lashed onto its tall, stable tines and combed through with a hand comb, then dizzed off into a sliver of combed top. The size of the hackle allows for more efficient processing of larger batches of fiber. They are priced in a similar range as hand combs, depending on pitch, maker, and accessories.

Experienced spinners may use these tools in tandem to process their fiber for specific results. For example, one might choose to comb the shorter fibers from a fleece before then carding it for a loftier spin, or to card fibers open prior to combing out any shorter bits. Adding a diz to the process of either carding or combing provides more options, creating rovings and slivers.

There are other, more "in between" ways to prepare your fiber for intentional spinning, such as hand-flicking locks with a small flicker brush or hand card, or flick-combing them against the teeth of the same.

Most spinners would classify flick-carding and flick-combing as falling somewhere "in between" a fully woolen to worsted result along the woolen to worsted spectrum.

Preparing fiber by hand takes dedication and time, though many spinners enjoy this aspect of handspinning as much as they enjoy the act of spinning the yarn itself.

I'm not going to tell you that the blending board makes haste of fiber preparation, but I think it offers a sense of play and a more casual approach to preparing colors, textures, and fiber preparations across the gamut. I 100 percent believe it's the most versatile equipment for fiber preparation available to the fiber enthusiast and that it's the best value for the money. This one tool has allowed me a greater exploration of my craft than any other. My blending board is my "desert island" processing tool—the one I couldn't be without. It works in harmony with household materials and specialty accessories, yielding most any resulting fiber preparation I can think of in my spinning pursuits.

Figure 1.22 Majacraft fine hand combs with smooth, blended fibers.

Figure 1.23 A flicker brush is a carding tool with firm-kneed teeth, used to gently tap open wool locks either for further processing or for spinning as is. Note the different card cloths and pin alignments in these three flickers.

Figure 1.24 Hand cards and flickers may be used similarly to open and/or semi-straighten locks of wool. While useful, many such flick cards are too harsh and rigid for use with your blending board.

	HAND CARDS	HAND COMBS/ HACKLE	DRUM CARDER	BLENDING BOARD
BEST SUITED FOR	Carding open and blending short to moderate-stapled fibers (commercial or fleece) and colors into tiny batts and fluffy single rolags; rolling punis	Combing locks of moderate to long lengths into alignment while removing short pieces; blends fiber (milled top or fleece) and smooth materials together	Blending/carding fibers (textures and colors) well; adding aeration and loft; batts and dizzed roving; color play	Carding rolags, punis, and puni-style rolags; dizzed and pulled roving/sliver; carding batts, adding layered effects; color blending and play, and textural elements; aeration of your fibers
OTHER USES	Flick-carding and flick-combing locks; dizzing roving; rolags may also be rolled from the short end of the paddle for a more aligned spin	n/a	Depending on the user's dexterity, roving may be dizzed. Some users are able to roll off rolags, too.	Thin layered effects for wet felting
OTHER ATTRIBUTES	A traditionally carded rolag made from fleece is considered the only truly woolen fiber preparation	Dizzing into a sliver after combing makes what's classically considered the truest worsted preparation	Fiber may be added in perpendicular or random layering, creating a true woolen preparation	Fiber may be layered in every conceivable angle and directional crossing
PROS	Portable and good for sampling ideas; useful for more than one type of preparation; affordable	Portable; can be lightweight; sometimes affordable, depending on size	Can last a lifetime; a practiced user can use the drum carder to create multiple results; easily scalable	Small footprint, breaks down easily for storage; transportable, cost effective, inexpensive (comparatively); ergonomic, adaptable for seated and standing use; capable of most any conceivable fiber preparation; fun to use, scalable results; takes most fleece and combed top equally well
CONS	Time consuming; holds a small amount of fiber per make	Larger pitch sets are heavy and may be dangerously sharp; time consuming; no extra uses	Expensive; large footprint; can cause repetitive stress injury and requires long stints of standing; time consuming; may require upkeep	Time consuming, albeit less so than larger carding equipment

Figure 1.25 Comparison of Fiber Equipment

Blending boards are portable and lightweight. They break down easily for safe storage in even the smallest of homes and are easily transported to classes, festivals, and gatherings. A blending board is designed to be kinder on the user's body and to avoid repetitive stress injury associated with a hand-cranked drum carder, and may be used in any part of the house and from a standing or seated position. I find the flat surface to be easier to work with than a round drum. I can place my fibers and my "mix-ins" exactly where I want them, making for scalable amounts of batts, rovings, and rolags, and I can obtain greater quantity in fewer makes than I could with a set of hand cards. By utilizing smaller sections, I can replicate the fluffiest of hand-carded rolags or a version of combed top that looks and acts as if it were truly hand-combed. Whatever I choose to make, my blending board sessions feel more like play than work. Best of all, I have excellent results with every type and blend of fiber I apply. As fiber-blending equipment goes, I wholly believe there's no better bargain than a blending board.

My carding sessions spark my creativity, while at the same time providing me a sense of calm.

The Woolen to Worsted Continuum

Fiber preparation falls anywhere from fully worsted to fully woolen on the other side of the spectrum, though most preparation falls along the range from woolen to worsted, in degrees, based on the traits associated with its processing. How you choose to spin such fiber also falls along the spectrum: A worsted spinning draw keeps twist out of the drafting zone; a fully woolen spinning draw allows the twist energy inside the drafting zone.

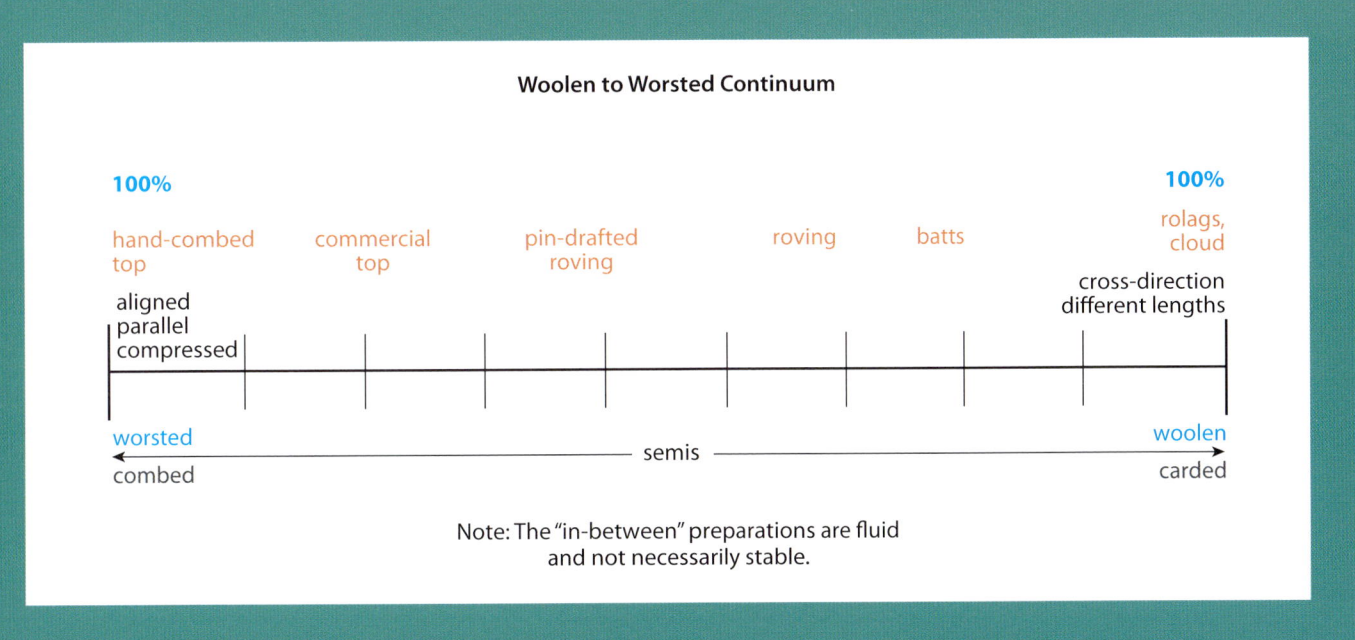

Note: The "in-between" preparations are fluid and not necessarily stable.

2

INDUSTRY SECRETS: UNLOCKING THE HIDDEN POTENTIAL OF YOUR BLENDING BOARD

By looks alone, the blending board was clearly designed for carding (and garneting), though its simplicity belies its potential for intentional fiber processing and preparation. Much like a blank canvas, this tool's adaptability relies on the user's imagination and techniques paired with the appropriate supplies needed to bring forth their vision. When working with a blending board, a spinner's fibers and mix-ins are their color palette, and their array of brushes, dizzes, and dowels are the mediums needed to yield intended results.

AFTERMARKET ACCESSORIES

To maximize the blending power of your blending board, you'll need to apply a few inexpensive aftermarket accessories to a thoughtful technique. These upgrades are easily purchased, though some may be lying unused in your home currently. All will vastly improve your process and outcome.

Brushes

The most important of these and the one that's central to your carding potential is your blending brush. This may be a true blending brush made with carding cloth or a household brush that works similarly to grip and hold your fiber strands extended for optimal carding. Without this tool, you're merely packing fiber down into your card cloth with no real change to its organizational or structural makeup. While this may be your goal on occasion, be aware that you can't achieve a fully carded-open, fluffed, and disorganized fiber without a proper brush for burnishing.

There are any number of brushes you probably have on hand that could work well with your blending board. I keep several in my own blending kit, as each works in its own way. To get the most effective carding and blending from your board, you'll need a brush with wire tines that are strong enough to open the fibers you're working with, without causing damage to them or the card cloth/tines underneath. Several makers now provide blending brushes with their blending-board kits, or you can purchase them separately from many online sources. However, even some kitted blending brushes are too harsh to use safely with your blending board. As mentioned in chapter 1, stay away from brushes with stiff, rigid wire teeth like (most) doffing brushes meant for use with a drum carder. These, and even some flicker brushes, are too harsh and can damage your tines and the foundation cloth itself. The makeup of carding brushes is as varied as our choices in blending boards and other carding equipment. Card cloth can differ in the density of its wire placement; tine length, firmness, and flexibility; foundation cloth makeup (materials, order of layering, and thickness); and the size, shape, curvature, workmanship, and materials of the paddle and handle. The cost of these specialty brushes can vary from just under $20 to more than $80. Here again, you may or may not be paying for workmanship and high grade of materials more than added utility, but a good carding brush will change the way you use your blending board.

Here too, labels don't always align with the product. Some makers include a large household paintbrush or a palm-sized, slim packing brush made of similar nylon bristles in their blending board packages and label this a blending brush. These can be useful for tamping down your layers of fiber and placing decorative elements, or even in helping to remove stray fibers from the cloth, but *these brushes don't card fiber.*

Household and beauty brushes (e.g., shoe-polishing brushes, hairbrushes, grooming brushes, even some kitchen utility brushes) can be exceptional blending tools, as can inexpensive pet slicker brushes—by nature their pins are soft and flexible. Look for brushes in the grocery or big box store with densely packed bristles in natural fibers (horsehair, boar bristles, etc.) or nylon, or other natural and synthetic materials. Choose a brush that's easy to grip. Two of my own favorites

Figure 2.1 Assorted brushes for carding and burnishing (those with wire tines) and for smoothing/tamping.

Figure 2.2 These different household brushes are excellent for smoothing your fiber and tamping it into place. They don't card fiber—at all.

Figure 2.3 These are two of my favorite multipurpose tamping brushes. I unearthed one in my bathroom drawer, and my neighbor was getting rid of the other. While their oval shapes are similar, the bristles are very different in density and stiffness, and thus, effect.

are oval and fit well in my palm, but their bristles are quite dissimilar. One is a soft horsehair that's excellent for tamping down fibers. The other, a brush meant for grooming horses, has stiffer synthetic bristles and a similar shape.

The more brushes in your blending toolbox, the more options you'll have for yielding specific results in your blending and carding, allowing you to use a single blending board to attain the results of multiple tools.

Dowels

While upgrading your brush selection will radically transform your blending board's carding capabilities, rethinking the dowels you use for rolling your fibers off the board can have a strong impact on your rolags and other roll-offs (chapter 3).

Dowels may be made from different woods and will often vary in finishing, if any. Dowel diameter varies among blending board makers, with most ranging in standard sizes of 0.5 (1.3 cm) to 0.875 inch (2.2 cm) in circumference. They're

Figure 2.4 These are some of the brushes and carders (household and fiber-specific) I use most with my blending board, including single hand cards with appropriately facing points. Each has somewhat different capabilities.

cut long enough for rolling off fibers up to the full width of your carding cloth and should be a few inches longer than your board's width to account for expansion in the fluffed, carded fiber, which begins to expand immediately upon removal if properly carded.

Your dowels may come completely unfinished, they may be sanded but otherwise unfinished, or even sanded, stained, and sealed with a wax or varnish. I prefer mine with a light satin finish, which makes it easier to slide the rods out from the roll-offs without damaging the tubes of fiber; but some roll-offs—notably punis—are easier to roll using a grippier, unfinished rod. With practice, all should work adequately in rolling off rolags, punis, and other roll-ups, and in picking up batts.

A thoroughly carded rolag will expand in girth and/or length after it's been rolled from the board and left to breathe for a few minutes, as air continues to circulate throughout its carded surface. The circumference or thickness of the dowels used influences the potential diameter of your rolled-off fiber tube. Rolling off using a 0.5-inch dowel can result in rolags or punis that are tighter than those rolled with a larger dowel—ideal for some situations. Using a fatter dowel to roll off a rolag offers the possibility for greater girth-wise expansion. Not only can a fatter set of dowels help you achieve a puffier rolled-off result, it can also make the rolling off process feel more comfortable, while a slimmer dowel can help you roll the thinnest of densely carded, short-stapled punis, all from the same blending board. The choice is yours.

The smoother the dowel, the easier it is to separate it from the roll-up without causing any visual damage to the delicate tube of fiber. This is where the wood's finishing may come into play. If you're rolling off with an unfinished dowel or dowels and your rolags feel like they're sticking to the wood when you're trying to remove them, try sanding the dowel(s) using a fine-grit sandpaper

Figure 2.5 These dowels all came with my blending boards, yet they're made from different types of wood, cut to different lengths, and range in extent of finishing and diameter.

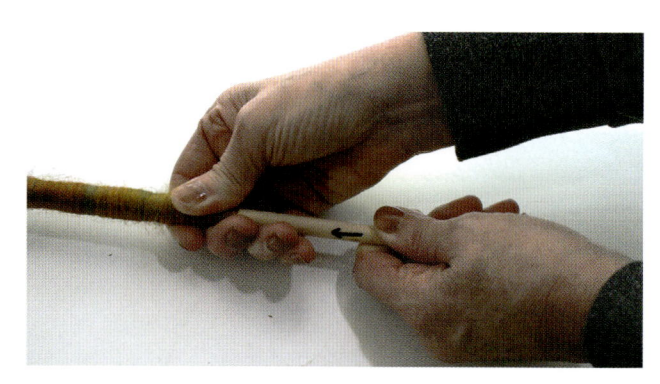

Figure 2.6 Punis stick to my favorite (unfinished) puni-rolling dowel when I try to remove them from the "wrong" direction. Marking the dowel with an arrow in the direction of the wood grain has alleviated the problem.

(150 grain) or testing for grain direction and marking the dowel accordingly (see figure 2.6). It's easier to push the puni or rolag off the dowel in the same direction as the grain vs. working against it.

Wooden dowels cost just a few dollars at the local hardware store, and collecting a selection of circumferences and even finishes can further stretch your blending board's potential. Metal dowels are a good option, too, and are just as easy to locate and have cut. Large-gauged wooden or plastic knitting needles can also work here, though most standard knitting needles are not long enough to use with a full board width's worth of fiber. (You can always load a narrower section of your blending board instead of its full width to get around this issue.) You may have other alternative dowels or rods at home. I find metal knitting needles to be too slick to use as single dowels, but they can be useful in a double-dowel roll-off (chapter 3). I've even seen spinners use chopsticks to roll their punis.

Dizzes

Adding a diz to your accessories kit will help you take your blending board to the next level with customized rovings. The diameter(s) of the hole/holes or slots in your diz will dictate the width of the fiber strip pulled through, so the more options you have, the better. (Note that these slots or holes will look smaller than you may have expected.

That's because friction is needed between the diz and the fiber to draw the fibers into a level of alignment and make a better roving.) Dizzes are made from all kinds of materials—wood, plastic, brass, and other metals, and even clay or bone, and all are relatively inexpensive. They may be concave in the center, but that's not an absolute—especially when you're just starting out. You likely have a perfectly good starter diz hiding at home. The plastic cover inside a spice jar served as my first diz for years, until I wore it out from use. A quarter-sized metal washer can make another good and cheap diz, but one of my own long-running favorites is a large round, concave, coconut shell button I bought as a memento of the first out-of-state blending boards class I ever taught. It holds special meaning and works well, too. I use a tiny crochet hook or wire-loop orifice threader to thread the diz when needed, if I don't have a dedicated threader handy. Whichever diz you go with, choose one that's lightweight. *Not all materials are equal.*

Figure 2.7 My favorite dizzes are made from wood, brass, and ceramic, while a spice jar top and quarter-sized washer still make for excellent starter dizzes. Clockwise from top center: brass diz from Wind Wools, New Zealand; plastic spice jar lid; walnut diz by Gregory Pencheff Woodturning; metal washer; coconut button; and clay diz by Charan Sachar/Creative with Clay.

Miscellaneous Supplies and Mix-ins

Miscellaneous items to keep on hand include a pair of sharp scissors and a reliable scale for weighing your materials when needed. Most people use a digital scale for weighing their fiber and mix-ins to ensure they can replicate their blends and results (figure 2.8). It's also helpful to keep a notebook—virtual or paper—for the same reason. Of course, you'll need your choice of wool/protein fiber(s) in the forms of combed top, roving, and/or scoured fleece, in addition to an array of what I call "mix-ins." These might be smooth and shiny, like processed Tencel or bamboo and other cellulose fibers; tussah, eri, peduncle, and other silks; nylons, firestar, and other synthetics, etc. You may also want to try working with more textured mix-ins, such as sari silk threads, silk noil, banana fiber, and recycled waste threads, handspun and weaving thrums, yarn scraps, various locks, Angelina, or even luxury fibers such as alpaca (and other camelids), angora, etc. The only add-in I (mostly) avoid is commercially milled sari silk roving. It's beautiful and convenient, yes, but sometimes the dyes in the silk scraps run once they get wet. This might not be significant if paired with dark wool and fully disseminated through the carded fiber, so I do occasionally use it—just sparingly, as a little goes a long way. Regardless, I prefer to control the colors, materials, and the amount of texture I add to my own blends.

Fiber play has become so popular among spinners in recent years that hand-dyers have begun offering pre-sorted scrap packs of various wool breeds and blends. These can serve as a great starting point for your blending board experimentation. They're fun to play with and take some of the guesswork out of color grouping. They allow the user to experience how breeds with differing staple lengths work on the blending board, together or separately, and to experiment with different color-play theories including gradients, color blocking, striping, and heathered yarns. The one problem here, if it is one, is that you won't know the exact identity of the wools and blends you're working with, but you'll surely have fun.

Figure 2.8 Sharp scissors, a scale, and an array of fiber mix-ins will prove invaluable in your blending adventures.

Figure 2.9 This scrap pack from Edgewood Garden Studio contains color-coordinated bits and bobs of hand-dyed fibers and smooth/shiny blendables.

Figure 2.10 Mix-in options are endless. Shown are some of my own favorites: dyed and undyed wool and mohair locks, all sorts of shinies (silks, nylon, bamboo, etc.), and textures galore.

Figure 2.11 I keep my mix-ins sorted in clear-topped locking and stackable plastic organizing bins of all sizes, for easy access. These bins are inexpensive and available at any big box or hardware store, and they simplify my process.

TECHNIQUE: DOS AND DON'TS

Your technique in loading your blending board matters just as much as the accessories and ingredients you pair with it. The joy of spinning carded fiber is its fluffiness and drafting ease, but a couple of common mistakes can keep users from enjoying the blending board's fullest carding potential. One of the most common is laying the fiber down in too-thick layers. Properly carded fiber is light and attenuates easily, and it starts with careful application to the blending board, just the same as when working with other carding equipment. (Please bear in mind that your process will speed up as your experience with your blending board increases, but fiber preparation is, by nature, a deliberate process.)

Pre-fluff Your Fiber by Teasing It Open

Take the time to fluff your fiber, whether from combed top or fleece, *before* putting it on the blending board. Teasing it open is your job, not the card cloth's. This goes for your main wool fiber and even your mix-ins. I like to utilize what I refer to as a "tease and whip" for hand-dyed commercial top, especially, which tends to compact from the dyeing process and then from sitting on its own weight in storage: Gently tease open a length of the fiber to its fullest width, then snap it in the air several times, using a strong whipping motion. You should see the fiber puff up more with each step. Whip the strip a few times or more. Turn the strip around, tease it open, and whip the other side. This forces air into the sheaves of fiber that were organized, aligned, and pressed together during commercial processing. I've yet to meet the (unfelted) commercial top that couldn't be saved with this trick.

Figure 2.12 Dyed Rambouillet top, unbraided.

Figure 2.13 Top teased widthwise.

Figure 2.14 Top after being "whipped," or forcefully snapped in the air several times.

Figures 2.15 and 2.16 Comparison of before (bottom and right, respectively in photos) and after (top and left) compacted fiber has been "teased and whipped" and its irrefutable results. Notice how much air has been returned to the fiber.

Layer Lightly and Purposefully

If you've ever taken a course in drum carding, you know that it takes time and patience to properly tease open the fibers and feed them into the carder and that the more care you put into separating and fluffing the fibers open beforehand, the better the results. Think about this concept when loading your blending board. Laying down thick clumps of unfluffed fiber leads to chunky and hard-to-spin rolags, rovings, and batts. Instead, lay your fiber down in thin staple lengths by allowing the surface of the board to work against the weight of your palm or fingertips as you attenuate.[8] This sounds painstaking, but it isn't at all once you get the feel of the movement. This also means that your layers of fiber build up gradually, and sparse areas will fill in organically as you continue to build up the board. Working from the top of the board down to the bottom builds natural sheaves of stacked fiber (think: roofing shingles) that will card open easily, as does working across it horizontally, also in rows.

Figure 2.17 Layer your fiber lightly using the pressure of your palm against the board to release the fiber in staple lengths. Working in rows (across or down the board) helps build a natural stacking order that fluffs and separates readily in carding and spinning.

---

8   The exception to this best practice is when you're specifically seeking a less carded, more worsted-like, result from your blending board. We'll cover this in chapters 3 and 4.

Figure 2.18 Hand-dyed Romney, hand-dyed Swedish Merino, Grey Romney, and Angora goat.

Figure 2.19 A flicker or blending brush can open fibers and release debris from fleece before blending.

Clean, fine to medium fleece may be used on your blending board, too; you're not limited to commercial top. Fleece/locks and top may be used together for unique results. Light VM is common, even in quality fleeces. If you have combs (a couple of inexpensive ones from the pet store will do), you can comb the debris out prior to loading the locks onto the card cloth, or use a flicker or blending brush to gently tap out the debris (figure 2.19).

Consider Directional Loading for More (and Less) Woolen Results and Other Effects

The action of carding, whether on a drum carder, hand cards, or a blending board, aerates the fibers while pulling them into something of an alignment against the rows of wire teeth. The carded fiber may then be spun with whatever draw the spinner wishes, to achieve a specific yarn. Carded fiber may be spun with a woolen draw, trapping as much air as possible; a worsted draw, compressing the yarn for a smoother but still somewhat airy result; or anywhere in between (see sidebar "The Woolen to Worsted Continuum," page 19). In more advanced carding, fibers may be loaded directionally, allowing the strands to cross in carding and spinning, thereby trapping a greater amount of air for a more woolen result with strands that are disorganized instead of aligned or nearly aligned. Fiber may be laid down randomly or perpendicularly—just so long as the staple directions will end up crossing. Adding layers or textural elements diagonally can help with "woolen-ness," while laying the strands and staple lengths down arbitrarily makes for an especially lofty result. The large, flat surface of the blending board makes directional and random loading simple, and the concept may be broadened further when combined with color effects and even wet felting.

Figure 2.20 Typical carding pulls strands of fiber into vertical alignment.

Figure 2.21 Laying your fiber perpendicularly allows more air to be trapped in between the layers and strands of fiber during spinning.

Figures 2.22, 2.23, and 2.24 Layering diagonally can better disperse your fiber than laying down horizontally, while laying your staple lengths arbitrarily is the most effective means of carding for maximum trapping of air and completely disorganized staple direction. Feel free to mix up these techniques in your layering.

Burnish Often

Use your preferred carding brush to burnish your layers often. This will help to open as many individual strands of fiber as possible for the most thorough blending of colors, textures, and your differing fibers. This also means that fewer strands and mix-ins will be left behind on the blending cloth when your fiber has been removed.

Use Your Scissors

When blending fibers that are greatly dissimilar in characteristics and/or staple length, you may want to cut the longer fiber(s) into lengths that better match the shorter one(s). This can also be effective when adding recycled materials like bits of yarn and thread, as the smaller surface areas will abrade more easily when burnishing, so they end up adhering to your fiber and yarn and not on your floor during spinning.

Figures 2.25, 2.26, and 2.27
Picking open and cutting your mix-ins down into small bits helps ensure a thorough blending throughout the rolag, batt, etc., as all facets are easily abraded.

Figure 2.28 The overhang of fiber at the base of your carding cloth is vital for rolling off punis, rolags, batts, and more. Don't skip it—ever.

Build Up an Overhang

When loading and burnishing your fibers, be sure to build up a suitable overhang at the bottom of the blending board. This fiber "shelf" is the starting point and stabilizer for every removal technique in this book.

Don't Fixate on Weight . . . Use It to Your Advantage Instead

Students always ask how much fiber their blending board holds, but there's not a singular answer to this question, nor is there a right one. If you've read this far, you know that card cloth from different manufacturers (made from differing TPI density, pattern openness, surface size, etc.) can hold differing amounts of fiber, even when cut to the same dimensions. A coarse, more open, carding cloth will hold more than a finer, denser cloth. Plus, a fine, toothy fiber has more density and takes up more space than a longer and denser silken one. Take the time to experiment with your blending board. I know that I can pack my full-sized 48 TPI blending-board cloth with up to 2 ounces of a dense and elastic fiber—an amount that corresponds to my similarly coarse, standard-size vintage drum carder. On the other hand, my fine, 108 PPI blending-board cloth holds the least amount of my lineup—right at 1.5 ounces of a fine fiber when fully packed. (Both boards have 11.5 in. x 11.5 in. [29.2 cm x 29.2 cm] cloths.) I prefer to make my loading and carding decisions based on the results I'm seeking. To make the very fluffiest rolags on any of my blending boards, for example, I underfill them. This allows the fiber to fully fluff open when carding, as the carding teeth can penetrate and aerate through the entire surface of fiber. When the rolags are rolled off, they will then expand up to double their initial length, depending on the fibers used and the rolling technique I employ (see chapter 3 for details). Underfilling is also better for the longevity of your blending board, as the mechanics associated with rolling and pulling rolags or puni-style rolags when the fiber has been too densely packed into the cloth and tines can ultimately put wear on the metal tips and even the foundation cloth itself.

My decision-making is entirely different when I'm carding for a batt or a slick and fragile roving. In both cases, I need to pack the fiber far more densely so the batt and/or roving will hold itself together once removed from the board.

Truthfully, I don't always weigh out my fibers, especially when I'm carding and spinning for my own enjoyment and experimentation. I do (pre-)weigh them out in batches when I'm recording ingredient amounts for replicating my recipes and results, and when I'm making rolags or other roll-offs for scalable color management in my spinning. This is when making roll-ups or batts in comparable weights matters more. To visually gauge how full your cloth is, just read the teeth from the side to see how high up the fiber is and whether there's room for more (figure 2.29). Your fingertips can also help to feel for sparse areas, which can be filled in as needed, as *these scant areas will be visible in any rolled-up preparation and make for weak areas in your roll-offs.*

Side view

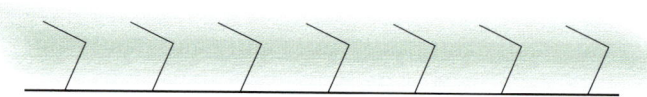

Figure 2.29 To visually gauge how full your cloth is, read the teeth from the side to see how high up the fiber is and whether there's room for more.

Don't forget to document your process for consistency in scalability. Making a digital or physical note in a designated area can be helpful, as can taking photos with your camera phone for quick reference.

Figures 2.30 and 2.31 I like to highlight what's inside my roll-ups by laying a few strands of shiny, sparkly, and/or other interesting elements down onto the card cloth before my main-ingredient wool.

Consider Your Order of Loading

This is important for rolags and other preparations that are rolled off the board. For most of us, our first layer of fiber becomes the exterior surface once that fiber has been rolled off the board into a cylinder shape. To create the most striking visual impact, I like to start my rolags and other roll-offs by first laying down a few strands of shiny, sparkly, or otherwise intriguing fibers. These also serve as a nod to the colors and textural bits inside the rolag. Light layers and adequate burnishing ensure that "shinies" and other such fibers adhere to my carded wool and *not* my carding cloth, leaving practically nothing behind. You may wish to highlight a rustic wool or some interesting texture or color in your fiber play.

Get Comfy with Your Blending Board

To combat fatigue, make sure to work with your blending board at a comfortable height and angle. Your arms should have full range of motion while you maintain good posture throughout the process. A blending board with a keel will usually have more than one angle position, so try them on for size. If I'm seated, I lay my blending board flat on my lap or keel it at a low angle held between my thighs, as resting it on a tabletop across from me feels too awkward from my seated position. Since I'm tall, most tables feel way too low for my height when I'm working while standing. Instead, I like to work with the board at chest level, atop my adjustable standing desk. If the board has a keel, I will sometimes lay the keel over the lip of my desk, securing it. If you prefer to work seated, be sure to rotate or place the board so it lies across your lap at a natural 45-degree angle. This allows your carding/burnishing arm to work ergonomically and without repetitive stress to it or your shoulder.

BEST PRACTICES IN LOADING YOUR BLENDING BOARD

- Lay down light, open layers, teasing open fleece/locks and combed top or roving, burnishing between the layers.
- Alternate layers between wool, "shinies," and other add-ins based on the degree of blending you're seeking.
- Use any breed and preparation of wool/fiber (and add-ins) that appeal to you, *except for* greasy, unscoured fleece.
- Use scissors to cut staple lengths of great variability into more similar lengths.
- When experimenting, you may want to sample a narrow area of your carding surface before committing to filling the whole blending board.
- Be sure to build up the overhang at the bottom of the card cloth.
- For loftier, lighter carded results, underfill the cloth. Alternatively, pack it full to ensure that a batt or roving blend will hold together once removed.
- Utilize directional layering to create a more woolen result.

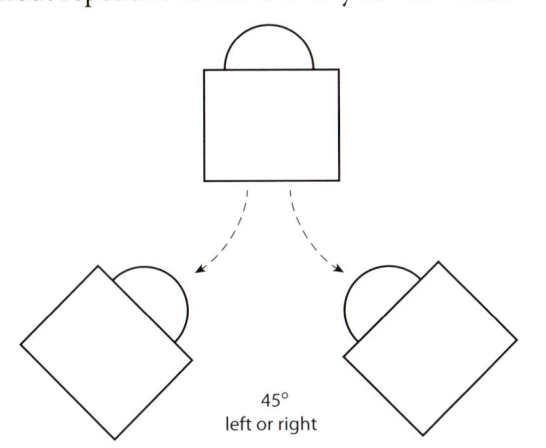

45°
left or right

Figure 2.32 If you work while seated, place the board so it lies across your lap at a natural 45-degree angle. This will allow your carding arm to work ergonomically.

MY FAVORITE WOOL BREEDS TO USE ON MY BLENDING BOARD

- Combed top in every short (1 in. to 3 in.) to medium-long (3 in. to 4 in.)[9] staple length, including, but not limited to: Rambouillet, Merino, Shetland, BFL, Falkland, Corriedale, Polwarth, Targhee, Finn, Down and Down-like breeds, and the above when blended with silk and/or bamboo, nylon, etc.
- CLEAN fleece/locks of all ilk
- Luxury fibers, including alpaca and other camelids, silks, cashmere, etc.

9 Slightly longer locks are great for more specifically combed-like processes and results.

SMOOTH VS. TEXTURED PREPARATIONS

The blending board is especially adaptable to almost any textural inclusion or design you can dream of. You may add texture to any of your blending-board preparations, though a textured dizzed roving will be limited by the size of the hole or slot in your diz. Texture, be it minimally seen or highly decorative, is a fun way to add pops of color and complex visual interest to both your carding and your finished spins. Depending on the openness of the patterning on your card cloth and/or its TPI, you can easily card in bolder, chunkier choices, too. I like to make tweeds from tiny bits of my own handspun scraps, but silks and banana fiber threads are other longtime favorites. Generally, we classify carded preparations as "smooth" when they have no such notable interruptive surface elements, but the lines between smooth and textured fiber preparation can be blurry. Light texture might be as subtle as a few strands of silk or processed flax, well-carded throughout your base fiber. If you're using leftover handspun or odds and ends of commercial yarns, keep in mind that lofty yarns and threads will adhere better than slick, compressed ones, no matter how small you cut them.

Figure 2.35 A collection of batts, rovings, and rolags in a range of smooth to textured blends.

Figures 2.33 and 2.34 I carded two batts using the same hand-dyed, commercial BFL, leaving the first one smooth (figure 2.33) and adding semi-teased, dyed mohair locks as texture to the second (figure 2.34). I made sure to leave the locks uncarded by tamping them into place.

Figure 2.36 Smooth batts (in process), carded from BFL.

At-home Garneting for Textural Inclusions

Garneting is a process in which textile scraps are rescued for reuse by shredding them down until the materials are returned to a fluffy and fibrous enough state to either be directly respun or blended/carded into another fiber. Industrially, this involves first machine-cutting the waste fabric, woven cloth, threads, and yarns into small pieces, which are then run through heavy-gauged machinery until returned to their original, completely broken-down state. The garneting board preceded the commercial process, much like a less refined version of today's blending board. The modern-day blending board allows for small-scale garneting at home, where you may put odds and ends of denim, leather, weaving waste, fiber scraps, and so on, through a similar process for reuse and/or inclusion in your spinning and your yarn design. In addition to helping stretch the value and use of our materials, garneting makes for beautiful tweed, color, and textural effects in our spinning. You could even garnet your scraps using hand cards before blending them into your

fiber on your blending board, or try using a single hand card or blending brush to garnet your inclusions *with* the blending board.[10] Blend the garneted inclusions into your main fiber afterward, or garnet and card these fibrous scraps together with your main fiber at the same time for a different outcome. Remember, the smaller the snippet or scrap, the better able you are to burnish it open on all facets, helping it to better adhere to the burnished strands of fiber.

---

10   Coarse cloth is ideal for this process.

Figure 2.37 I teased open and snipped extra lengths of handspun, dyed banana and silk threads, and dyed locks down into pieces no longer than half an inch and fluffed them open using just my fingertips.

Figures 2.38, 2.39, and 2.40 The fibers from figure 2.37 are not quite back to their original fibrous state, but they still blended perfectly into various breeds of commercial top, making for different tweed effects.

Not every blend or textural inclusion requires garneting. Much of your at-home carding will include lightweight, "soft," and malleable materials like noil, Angelina, and carding waste—all suitable for light texture—and these will readily blend into your base fiber so long as you've teased these bits open well and engage in the other "best practices" advised thus far. When working with locks, bits of fabric or yarn, etc., teasing the items open where appropriate and/or cutting them down into small pieces (figure 2.25 on page 32) allows for greater carding contact on all planes, without any extra processing first. However, if chunkier and less-thorough blending is your preference, leave your locks (feathers, ribbons, etc.) in larger strips or whole, and work them into your yarn in the spinning and plying processes.

Figure 2.41 Teasing locks and threads open to their thinnest strands helps them adhere better to your base fiber and to blend in more seamlessly, while working with larger-sized add-ins and fibers/colors yields a chunkier, more art batt–like, result.

Textural Inclusions You Might Want to Add to Your Own Stash

Sari silk threads, silk noil, banana threads, novelty yarns, carding waste, Angelina, firestar, assorted wool and mohair locks, bast fibers (flax, hemp, etc.) and cotton lint, stellina and other manufactured fibers, soy silk, weaving and spinning thrums, and scraps of fabric or ribbon.

Figure 2.42 Clockwise from top center: hand-dyed Rambouillet commercial top, ecru Dorset roving, Angelina sparkle, hand-dyed BFL top, dyed and undyed silks, hand-dyed fine to medium-stapled locks. These were all carded together on my $45, 90 TPI blending board (see appendix) and rolled into one single log from each make of the board. Each rolled log weighs half an ounce and took just a few moments to create.

WORKING WITH "DIFFICULT" FIBERS

What, exactly, is a "difficult" fiber? To me, these are fibers that are uniquely short-stapled, with surface textures unlike that of wool. They may feel slicker or have fewer or no surface scales, or they may just be vastly different from the spinning "norm" (for example, cotton or camel down). These types of fibers may require some kind of specialty carding or processing in order to spin them on their own and/or might be somewhat challenging to fully incorporate with other base fiber(s) like wool. Examples include (unprocessed) cotton; down undercoats including yak, musk ox/qiviut, bison, possum, and guacano; angora, cashmere, and certain other luxury fibers. These inherent differences typically result in these fibers being labeled "tricky" or "advanced," causing many spinners to feel uncomfortable using them. In truth, however, they can be used quite successfully in blending . . . You just have to make conscious choices and considerations when pairing them with other fiber(s).

A fine or superfine carding cloth and a woolen preparation is your best bet for fully incorporating a trickier fiber into your yarn in as few carding passes as possible, along with utilizing a base wool that's complementary in fineness and staple length.

Step 1: Hold a few strands of your luxury fiber between your fingertips and thumb, and coax them open before adding them to a layer of well-carded wool. Continue until you have a thin layer atop your wool base.

Step 2: Top with another layer of your base wool, and burnish well. You may want to card the batt a second time (chapter 4) before rolling it off into punis (chapter 3) if the fibers are especially short. No other specialty equipment is needed.

Figure 2.43 Alpaca roving is blended through a base of fine-stapled, green scrap wools.

3

ROLLED-OFF PREPARATIONS: ROLAGS, ROLLED LOGS, PUNIS, AND ROLY-POLIES

Most people think of rolags when they think of the blending board, but the rolags we blend and make on the blending board tend to be smoother and denser than those traditionally made with a pair of hand cards. This is from a combination of the larger carding surface and its longer teeth, the more direct carding action needed to fully open and blend your fibers on the board, and the typical manner of rolling off (see figure 3.2 for the full explanation), producing a tube of fiber that's more structurally aligned than a true, fully woolen rolag made with a pair of hand cards. However, with more awareness and adjustments to the methods and materials you use, you can create blending-board rolags that are *almost* identical in woolen-ness to a "true" hand-carded rolag—if that's what you're looking for.

Rolags may be the best-known blending board preparation, but they are only one potential tubular possibility we can create with this tool. There are also punis, rologs (aka rolled logs), and little buggers I like to call roly-polies. This chapter is designed help get your yarn design cylinders well . . . rolling.

Figure 3.1 "True" woolen rolags made from fine to medium fleece and snips of silk, using hand cards.

Figures 3.2 and 3.3 Rolling rolags off the blending board is typically done with a set of dowels, first clamping the overhang of fiber between them to get the rolling started. Physiologically, it's only natural to then pull down against the tines while rolling the tube up and off the card cloth to break it from the remaining carded fiber, attenuating the strands into alignment in the process. However, the user can manipulate the shelf prior to rolling for a more or less woolen effect. (Stay tuned!)

Figure 3.4 Hand cards are optimal for carding a "true" woolen rolag, but you can still get a fluffi-er-than-typical result with your blending board and the right application and roll-off technique. Can you tell which rolag is which? Answer: The hand-carded rolag is on the left; the blending board rolags—the first one rolled most typically— are to its right. Note that I used a fine, dense fiber for these rolags and my own DIY blending board made with Howard Brush's proprietary blending cloth to card the three rolags on the right and my 96-point Majacraft hand cards to make the true rolag on the left.

Figure 3.5 Bottom left to top right: Punis (2) carded and rolled from Ashford's 108 TPI blending board vs. (2) rolled using Majacraft's 140 TPI handcards. Both sets were rolled off using a traditional single dowel. The hand-carded punis have an airier, fuzzier surface.

ROLLED-OFF PREPARATIONS, DEFINED

Rolag

A traditional woolen rolag is made by carding light layers of fiber between two hand cards, with multiple passes. The small batt is then gently rolled longwise into a light-as-air, cigar-shaped cylinder. (It can also be rolled from the shorter side; but since the fibers would then spin in a more aligned manner, this isn't a traditional rolag.) When fleece is used, any short, uneven lengths will be directionally scrambled in the process, creating a fully woolen rolag. The same could be said about a rolag made from combining combed tops (commercially processed fiber) of different staple lengths and/or combined with textural elements of differing staple lengths.

Figure 3.6 shows East Fresian fleece (with tweed effect from randomly dyed bits of wool locks). The three rolags on the left were hand-carded fully woolen, using 72 TPI Leclerc hand-cards. The bundle on the right was carded and rolled from my DIY blending board made with "true" blending cloth at approximately 72 PPI. I rolled both groups using two dowels. In figure 3.7, I carded together hand-dyed Merino/silk (80/20) top, camel down, silk noil, firestar, and banana threads using my 96 TPI Majacraft hand cards (leftmost rolag) and again, my DIY blending board (middle and right puni-rolags). I added a slightly loftier effect to the middle version by rolling it with fatter dowels than the one on the right.

Figures 3.6 and 3.7 A traditional, fully woolen rolag is carded with and rolled from a set of hand cards, optimally using clean locks of varied lengths, though plenty of spinners use commercially processed top for their rolag-making. Hand-carded rolags are considered lighter and airier than those rolled from a similarly clothed blending board . . . or are they?

Figure 3.8 These rolags are similarly lofty and light, though they are made with commercial top and not locks. Believe it or not, one is made with a 72-point set of hand cards, while the other is carded and rolled from my blending board. The answer to which is which lies in the background of the photo, where the respective tools line up with each of the practically identical rolags.

Puni

A puni is also traditionally hand-carded, but it's denser than a rolag. Historically, punis are made from the shortest of fibers (1 inch or less), notably cotton, but fine and/or luxury fibers can be used alone or in blended combinations to make punis, and even a well-carded, shortish staple length fiber (up to approximately 2 inches long) can make a nice puni, too. Once carded, the dense batt is rolled up tight using a single thin dowel or knitting needle. Punis travel and keep well due to their firmer form. They yield a finely spun yarn.

Note: While longer staples will also appear to card and roll up nice and tight and will look just like any other puni from the outside, these are not optimal since the longer strands tend to tangle together as the fibers are pulled from the slightly twisting center of the cylinder during spinning.

Figure 3.10 Bottom to top: hand-carded rolag, puni-style rolags (3), and punis (2). The puni-rolags and punis were made on the blending board. Note that I used a fine, dense, hand-dyed fleece combined with commercial silks/shinies and my own DIY blending board made up of 90-point carding cloth.

Figure 3.9 Two different ways to roll a puni: Traditionally, punis are rolled using a single dowel or knitting needle, but using a set of knitting needles and what I like to call "kissing the cloth" yields nearly identical results. I've used a 0.5-inch diameter dowel for the top four punis and a set of size US 7 knitting needles to roll the three below them.

Puni-rolag

Some traditionalists would call the typical blending board rolag a "puni-style" rolag, or puni-rolag, and I don't disagree. Most spinners tend to pull on the dowels firmly, attenuating the carded fibers into more alignment as they're rolling from the board. It also tightens the tube, creating a "rolag" that falls somewhere in the middle of a true rolag and its tighter puni cousin. However, we can make up for this added attenuation—or avoid it altogether—by using the tips and tricks to follow in this chapter, and/or by approaching the loading of the board and removal of the fiber with a more woolen result in mind.

Rolog (aka rolled log)

I first heard this term used by Beth Lower of the former Blue Mountain Handcrafts. Instead of rolling multiple rolags off your board, you roll one single fat cylinder, resembling a rolled log, using the whole board's worth of carded fiber. You can then spin directly from one end of the log so the fibers spin into a jumbled, woolen delight, or you can gently pull the fiber into a roving first, which will be covered in the next chapter.

A single rolled log (or even two smaller ones) is the easiest of all roll-offs, as its expanse allows for double-dowel removal that lies somewhere between a rolag and a batt, leaving its cylindrical wall as light and lofty as possible.

---

11 I wanted to name this mini after the Jewish cookie of my childhood, Rugelach, but I was worried that the pronunciation might be intimidating to those who've never heard of these "small twists"—the approximate Yiddish translation. Plus, "roly-poly" better fits the category. No matter what you call them, definitely try these little rolls!

Figures 3.11 and 3.12 All roll-ups, including these large rolags, can be spun from the end or hand-pulled or dizzed into a roving before spinning.

Roly-poly[11]

These small delights can resemble a rolag, puni, or puni-rolag in characteristics. They're effective for sampling blends of breeds and/or colors, and even more so for specific color play results. They're not good for high textural inclusion as the surface area is too small.

Figure 3.13 Use just a small segment of your board to make a roly-poly or two.

Figure 3.14 Roly-polies are great for sampling and color play.

All of the above preparations belong to the grouping "roll-offs," meaning that a dowel, or more commonly a set of dowels, is used to remove the fiber from the blending board. Your approach to this rolling action also simultaneously shapes your particular rolled-off preparation. With practice and foresight, you can manage the degree of woolen-ness attainable in the end product.

ROLLING FIBER OFF YOUR BLENDING BOARD

You will need a set of dowels and a household paintbrush and/or a gentle cleaning or blending brush for these roll-offs.

Either of the following methods may be used to create and remove your rolag, puni, puni-rolag, rolled log, or roly-poly from the blending board, depending on the result you're seeking. This is where the all-important fiber overhang from chapter 2 comes into play. Please note that I am using the term "dowel" as a general term for the appropriate smooth rod(s) referenced in chapter 2. You may substitute knitting needles, chopsticks, etc. in the diameter and material that works best for you, based on the preparation you're removing/rolling and the size, degree of woolen-ness, etc., you're seeking. When rolling multiple rolags from one make of your board, have an idea of how many you can roll evenly, as this can affect your color management in spinning, if that matters to you. This does take some familiarity with your particular blending board and its card cloth. Pre-weighing batches of your fibers and any mix-ins can also be helpful here, especially when combined with the measuring tape hack shown in figure 3.16.

Figure 3.15 I keep a thick and gentle household paintbrush or a soft tamper next to my blending board when I'm ready to roll off. These are useful for coaxing any few lagging fibers from the card cloth as I begin to roll off.

Figure 3.16 I don't want to permanently mar my blending board(s) with ink or notches, so instead I attach a cloth measuring tape to my board using a binder clip or clamp when experimenting with new blends and color play. The measurements can be helpful when trying to roll off rolags in somewhat equal proportions. A homemade paper or cardboard template will work just as well.

Easier still . . . just make a single lightweight rolog per each make of your board. The fewer roll-ups you roll from each make, the easier it is to keep their weights and makeup as close to the same as possible.

Double-dowel Roll-off

Whether I'm standing or sitting, I prefer to roll my rolags with my blending board in its usual straight-up form, without swiveling it upside down. I find this gives me the best level of control. Some people prefer to swivel their board to the upside-down position before rolling—so the rolling off starts at what becomes the top of the swiveled board—for a different angle of release off the tines. You may roll under or overhand from this position, but bear in mind that rolling under-handed will turn your *top* layer of fiber into the rolags' exterior, not the bottom layer. Experiment to find your preference. For me, making effective use of loosening the fiber overhang "shelf" at the base of the card cloth adds a far greater degree of control in rolling off, eliminating the need to turn or swivel the unit, but again, this is a personal choice. There are two exceptions:

1. If your blending-board tines aren't blunted at the tips for safety, then I would recommend turning your board upside down for your roll-offs—especially when rolling punis with a single dowel. This is a safer angle to work from to avoid injury and cuts to your knuckles and hands, just the same as when rolling rolags when working with a set of sharp-tined hand cards.[12]

2. When rolling punis, as elaborated further under "single-dowel roll-offs," below.

Rolling Off with Two Dowels

Step 1. Using both hands and working from the two sides inward, *firmly* "snap" the overhang upward, lifting it up slightly from the bottom row or two of teeth, thus releasing it for further removal. This helps the fiber roll up as one unit, leaving fewer strands behind. *The initial amount of fiber lifted off the carding teeth can also help you control the degree of loft in your rolled preparation.* This head start means that you won't need to pull down against the tines and tighten the tube as much to break it off from the rest of the fiber supply. For a more woolen roll, lift the fibers up about an inch or so before rolling (right in photo). (Repeat this with each roll-off from the same make of the board.) For a more aligned roll-off, just barely release the overhang (left in photo). For an even more aligned, puni-like roll-up, tug down on the fiber supply after release, lightly engaging the nearest teeth.

Step 2. Clasp the full length of the overhang between your dowels, keeping them off-center from each other (this makes their removal much easier). Make sure the entire length of your fiber

---

12 Wearing silicone finger sleeves (available online) is another way to protect your knuckles, if you prefer.

shelf has been captured between the dowels before you start rolling and adjust if needed.

Step 3. Start rolling, slowly and gently. For the more woolen rolag, try not to attenuate, or pull down on, the dowels and fiber as you're rolling. The action here is to roll and roll, then pull to tear from the fiber supply. For a more aligned and denser puni-rolag, go ahead and pull down while rolling, tensioning the weight of your fiber against the tines. The action for the latter is pull and roll, pull and roll. Experiment with the rolling/pulling order until you've got the roll-off you're seeking. No matter what, be prepared to break off the rolag (roly-poly, etc.) at a natural point, especially when you're rolling a puni-rolag. These tend to become dense when rolled too thick. If you're rolling multiple rolags/puni-rolags from one make of your blending board, consider how many you can get from the board so they're as close to even weight-wise as possible.

The coarser the carding or blending cloth, the loftier your rolls will be, without much effort on your part. The size of your dowel will also affect the number of rolags you get from each make of

the board, as will the fibers used, the size of the card cloth, how lightly or how densely you roll off, etc. Counting the number of rolls before each break is a good way to ensure your puni-rolags and other rolls are close to the same weight (e.g., roll three times, then break the fiber, roll three times again, break, and so on). Should you note any strands of fiber lagging behind the rest, gently coax them back into the mix using your fingertips or your paintbrush. A gentle blending brush may be substituted, held so the points of its tines pick up the fiber instead of pushing it down deeper between the teeth on the blending board cloth.

To roll a more woolen rolag, rolog, etc., pre-release the fiber as shown on the right side of step 1 and roll without attenuating against the tines of the card cloth.

If need be and while the roll is still on the dowels, "tickle the tines" ever so lightly with the outer edge of your rolag or log, etc. for a neat edge appearance and to make sure it's sealed closed.

Step 4. Carefully remove the dowels, being sure to avoid pulling on your rolled-up fiber as a fluffy rolag is especially prone to damage. Remove one rod, then the other. I like to gently loosen the first rod by twisting it back and forth lightly, then carefully sliding it out from the bottom or up from the top, respectively. To remove the rolled-up fiber tube without damage, I then push it up and off the second dowel, making sure my grip is just beneath the base of the roll first. You may remove the dowels in either order.

Clamping the overhang and rolling with the rods or dowels offset from each other makes their removal easier. For added assurance, don't roll too tightly.

For this move, gently roll the very outer edge of your roll-up against the wire pins in a slight combing motion, sealing the tube closed and smoothing out the rough edge in the process.

Step 5. Repeat all the steps until finished, avoiding the very top row of tines and their carded waste as these can add a messy look to your rolled preparations. (This is much less apparent when using a coarser card cloth and certain fibers.)

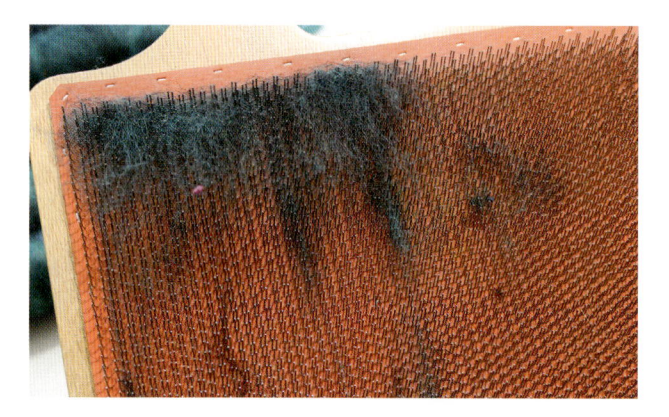

Use a cleaning brush or an upside-down blending brush to carefully remove the carding waste and put it aside to use as future mix-ins.

Step 6. "Kiss the cloth" (optional) for a fuzzier, loftier roll-off. This is my favorite trick, and you won't believe the results it produces. I liken this action to lawn aeration, where patterned holes are poked down into the soil, allowing its surface to breathe. Take your rolled-off rolag or puni-rolag and center it at the base of your card cloth. Using both palms, *gently* roll it up, rolling-pin style. (Always roll up, not down, or you can damage the surface fibers of your work.) You will see the tube of fiber begin to expand immediately as the tines perforate down into the hollow tube of fiber, allowing more air to flow through. You may repeat the process as many times as you'd like but remember that each pass will make the outer surface fuzzier in appearance, so if maximum sheen is your goal this may not be the tip for you. Put your rolag to the side of your work surface and let the fibers continue to expand. Results will vary based on the usual multitude of fiber and card cloth–related factors, but my own puni-rolags and rolags often easily double in length. This is also a great save for anything that rolls off more densely than you'd wanted.

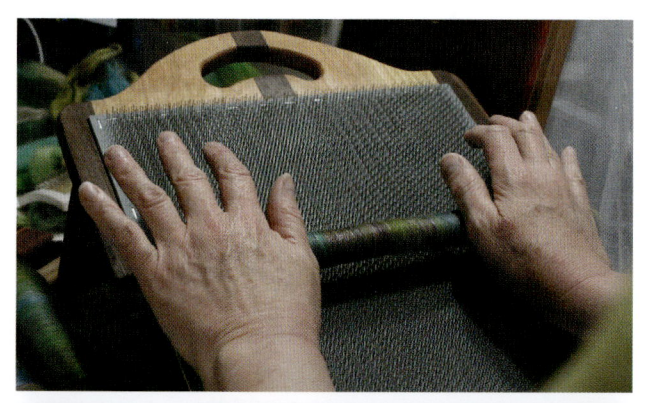

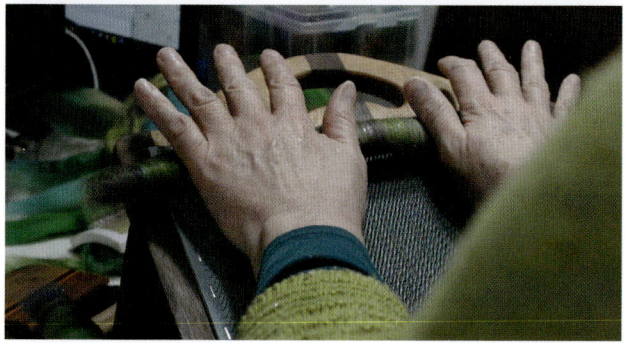

Each set of fine-fleece puni-rolags (bottom two) and punis (top two) is shown with and without kissing the cloth. The longer of each pair is the one that kissed the cloth. Both pairs began as identical rolls.

Some professionals use scissors to trim and clean up the edges of their rolags and roll-ups as needed. Be careful not to over trim, which can create uneven staple lengths you'll need to address while spinning your singles. I've trimmed the left sides of the heathered grouping, which was made from commercial top.

Single Dowel Roll-off

A single dowel is traditionally used to roll a puni—a denser and tighter version of a rolag.[13] You'll want to use shorter fibers (about an inch or less in staple length) for best results in spinning these tighter rolls. Clean, fine fleece works beautifully, as do luxury fibers like alpaca, yak, bison, and musk ox, and cottons and other cellulose fibers, which may be blended together and/or with wool for lovely results. When using the very shortest downy fibers with a staple length well below an inch, a fine carding or blending cloth utilized with a dense brush will provide the best, most thoroughly blended, results. When using the traditional single dowel to roll your puni, it's best to turn your blending board upside down for maximum efficiency and tube aeration. Here, a dowel with a touch of grip works best to help get the rolling started. I like a sanded, unfinished dowel, but a lightly varnished dowel works too, since this adds a bit of tackiness to the wood's surface. Due to their density, punis are less fragile to work with than rolags, but the first roll-off can be finicky to get started. Since you'll be using a single dowel or rod and your hands as your roll-off tools, you will be working more closely and more directly with the teeth of your blending board and engaging their aerating action against the fiber, even as you attenuate. Punis are wonderfully airy for this reason and make an ideal preparation for woolen spinning. Exercise caution when starting the first roll-up, to avoid cutting your skin against potentially sharp tines.

---

13 Using two fine- to medium-gauged knitting needles or a pair of chopsticks instead of a single dowel or single knitting needle can also provide excellent results with toothy, fine, and otherwise appropriate fiber for carding and spinning punis, though this will alter the arrangement of the fibers.

Step 1. Turn your blending board so it's bottom up. Loosen the fiber overhang, lifting it from the first rows of tines.

Step 2. Lay your dowel (knitting needle, chopstick, etc.) down on the loosened shelf of fiber. Pull the entire edge of the fiber up and over your dowel, toward you.

Step 3. Once you've secured the entire edge, start rolling toward you, using the wire tines to help lock the fibers into place as you roll. Lift the dowel and puni-in-progress up from the card cloth enough to detach it from the rest of the fiber, still rolling as you do so, engaging the teeth if needed. The less fiber you've got on your blending board, the tighter and thinner you can pull and roll your punis, if that's what you're seeking. (If you're using the longer range of recommended fiber, between

one and two inches in staple length, don't roll too tightly.)

Step 4. Continue until you've reached the other end of the board, avoiding the rough card waste on the final row(s) of teeth. Carefully remove the waste using a cleaning brush or an upside-down blending brush. Put this aside to use as future mix-ins.

Step 5. Kiss the cloth (optional, see step 5, *Double-dowel Roll-off* on page 50).

Both punis were rolled up and off with a traditional single dowel. The upper puni was then kissed against the cloth, creating a fuzzier surface and more expansion than the bottom one.

Make It More Woolen

A true, 100 percent woolen preparation is made of carded fibers of varied lengths with disorganized direction, with strands that cross vertically and horizontally when spun. The amount of aeration varies with your choices of wool, the characteristics of your blending board's carding cloth, the brushes you use, and, of course, your technical approach throughout, including application and removal. In addition to applying the best practices in loading your blending board shown in chapter 2, use any or all of the following tips to maximize the woolen effects in your fiber.

Make It More Woolen: Tips for the Fattest, Fluffiest Rolls

Underfill your board. Underfill your board considerably, but still evenly. I like to use anywhere from 1/3 to 2/3 of the amount of fiber my board would normally hold if fully packed, though I usually rely on a visual assessment or my scale. This keeps the carded preparation light and allows for a greater degree of control when rolling off the board. The same premise still holds true, even if you're working with filling a smaller section of the blending board.

Manipulate your overhang shelf for desired impact. Lift up the overhang at the base of your board, releasing it an inch or so off the tines. This head start in rolling means you won't need to pull against the board's teeth as you roll the rolag.

When rolling off, use a fatter dowel or set of dowels to accentuate the loft already created.

Roll fewer rolags from each make of the board and try to attenuate as little as possible while doing so.

Consider the fiber. Shorter, fine fibers and fibers with "grab" to them (Targhee, CVM, Merino, Polwarth, Rambouillet, most Down and Down-like breeds, and more) will naturally have a fuzzier surface appearance to them than longer, more lustrous ones and will spring open more visibly once the fiber has been burnished.

An assortment of hand-dyed locks with various natural traits of grab, length, crimp, sheen, etc.

Use a mix of scoured locks/fleece and commercial combed top.

Load your fibers directionally so the strands cross and scramble during carding. These cross-directional layers keep some separation between the layers of fiber, allowing more air to get trapped between them during carding and spinning. You may load perpendicularly, as shown in chapter 2, diagonally, or randomly for atypical results.

Load fibers in cross-directional layers for interesting woolen results.

Consider dowel size when carding and rolling longer fibers so the individual strands don't get twisted and tangled together while spinning, and/or try using a single large-circumference rod or dowel, puni-style, for your roll-off, with your board in the upside-down position and allowing for full-surface, deep aeration of the fiber tube.

"Kiss the cloth" of the board by gently rolling your freshly removed roll-up from the base of the carding cloth upward to the top. If the rolag grows more than you'd like and you're concerned about how to store and/or handle it when spinning, just cut it in half, into two tubes.

Make It (Slightly) More Worsted

By their cylindrical nature, it's not possible to make a worsted rolag, puni, or other rolled preparation, but attenuating your fiber as you're rolling it off the board will pull your carded fibers into more of an alignment. Additionally, working with commercial top instead of fleece—especially longer, more lustrous blends and breeds such as Corriedale, BFL, Falkland, etc.—and blending it with nylon, silk top, and such (or buying or creating a blend containing bamboo, silks, nylon, etc.) will yield a smoother result with more sheen, especially in the finished yarn.

To roll off, lightly loosen the overhang at the base of your board by tugging the overhang toward yourself, *trying to not lift it up* (see the left side of Step 1 photo, "Rolling Off with Two Dowels," on page 47).

Clamp the bottom overhang between your dowels and pull down against the weight of the tines above your rolag, using them in more of a combing and aligning, rather than carding, action. For the very smoothest results, *try to minimize the rolag's contact with the tines beneath it while rolling to avoid added aeration and marring of its surface.* Use your thumbs against the board as added tension if need be.

Troubleshooting

No matter how you choose to lean into making rolags and other roll-ups, a few common problems tend to arise.

Why can't I break off my fiber where I want it? You probably haven't released enough of a working ledge, or overhang, from the grips of the card cloth. This needs to be done with each rolag, not just the first one. Think of spinning with your hands too close together . . . They need to be far enough apart for the fiber's strands to release and slide past each other. This is a similar concept.

My rolags and punis are uneven in circumferences/sizes. This still happens to me, too, especially if I'm not paying attention to my rolling.

Practice helps, as does counting your rolls. I now prefer to roll fewer rolags (no more than three) from each make of my underfilled board. This makes for easy sizing.

One of my rolags is much longer than others. That rolag ended up with less fiber in it than the others, most likely from a sparse area while you were carding and filling your card cloth. This area will card open more visibly than the thicker-laid areas.

Why are there thin spots in my rolled log/ rolag? Most likely, there were sparsely filled areas on your carding cloth, which is prone to happen when we underfill our blending board. To check for these spots, hold your board up to the light at an angle, prior to rolling off, to check for shadowy areas. Don't forget to also check your outer edges by looking at the tines from the side, as these outer areas tend to get overlooked. It's also possible that you've got a damaged or bent tine, so check your board to see if any of the wire teeth are bent or out of alignment with the others. If you find a bent tine, you can ease it back into place with the help of a hollow mechanical pencil (see *Care and Storage of Your Blending Board*, chapter 6).

My rolags are too thick and dense. This could be any number of issues, or even several of them at once. Consider the following:

- Try loading less fiber onto the board, making certain to fully fluff your fiber open widthwise prior to laying it onto your blending board. Dyed commercial top is especially prone to compaction. Gently tease it open widthwise down the length of the strip, then whip the strip in the air sharply, multiple times. Turn the strip around, tease it open, and whip air into this side, too. This maneuver forces air in between the sheaves of fiber stacked together during commercial processing. It will be as good as new—or better.

- Lay the fiber down on your board in wispy-light staple lengths by using the weight of your fingers or palm to hold it in place with one hand and releasing the layers with the other.

- Don't forget to loosen and/or lift the fiber overhang before roll-off, unlocking it from the wire tines. (Do this for the beginning of each rolag, though you won't need as much of an overhang when working your way up the board.) This should allow you more control over deciding where to break off the fiber.

My rolags are too hard to roll—making them is an upper-body workout! You've got too much material on your blending board. Try using less fiber or rolling a single rolled log instead.

COLOR, TEXTURE, AND OTHER CREATIVE PLAY

Roll-ups provide an easy and excellent means for anyone looking to get to know their blending board and its potential. You can keep things simple and just enjoy spinning your wooly preparations, or you can implement a more intentional color and/or textured effect as your confidence grows. The following are some basics to get you started on planning the yarn you want to spin. *These and other creative effects may be applied to the preparations in both chapters 3 (roll-ups) and 4 (batts and roving).* Even better, combine these processes in your spinning!

Flecks, Tweeds, and Heathers

Flecks, tweeds, and heathers are all related effects but with different historical meanings, plus some overlap. Today, tweed is simply a fabric with blips of differing colors and/or a nubby texture to it, usually in the form of small flecks of color or textured bumps. A tweeded texture can be seen and felt on its surface, while a heathering is more of a blending of the background colors. A heathered yarn may also include the nubby flecks of color or texture most of us would call tweed, merging the concepts. All lend elegance to their fabric.

Tweed is not just a classic look. It originated as a wool fabric designed hundreds of years ago by the farming people of Scotland, who made full use of local wool scraps to spin and weave a weatherproof cloth to stave off the cold, windy, and wet outdoors environment in which they worked. It just so happens that the nubby or otherwise color-speckled look of the cloth is timeless and sophisticated. The fiber is carded and spun fully woolen, both historically by hand and still today by machine. The process creates a fabric that's uniquely warm and waterproof, as the coast of Scotland has dank weather and its residents worked almost exclusively outdoors to sustain themselves and their hard-to-reach islands.

Tweed is still in production there to this day, with colors harkening to the magnificent Scottish landscape and its rich history, while spinners worldwide borrow from the nubby and/or color-specked theme for the sake of its beauty and its sustainability. The slubby feel may be barely incorporated, and the color theme may be as subtle or as daring as the spinner desires. There are any number of ways to put a tweed-style handspun yarn to use, even in one's knitting or crochet, and not just in weaving.

Make Your Own Tweed Blend

Remember that the scope of the colors and degree of texture is your call. You could choose a "barely there" inclusion of neutral or natural-colored wool remnants or go full-out wild with your speckles and nubs. As with any such endeavor, make sure to consider your project and its end use when selecting your materials, and be sure to sample before diving all in.

Step 1. Gather your mix-ins. You need only a minimal amount of scraps—a gram or two of scraps goes far for most of us.

Step 2. Tease open your mix-ins until they're broken down into their smallest, lightest strands. If needed, garnet them open using your blending board and a good carding brush. For a true speckled result in your knitting, you want to blend small *blips* of color into your main fiber— not longer *stripes* of color. However, you can get away with carding somewhat longer color runs if a) you're chain-plying the yarn (thus shortening the length of that color in the finished skein) or b) you're using the yarn for weaving, where the interlacement of warp and weft affords a longer length of color or texture.

The top leftmost fiber resulted in a tweedy or speckled yarn, while the bottom rightmost fibers produced the center yarn, which has longer, bolder pops of color and is less tweedy and more stripey.

Step 3. Lay down a light layer of your main fiber and burnish it. Add your flecks, lightly tamping into place, and card. Continue layering/burnishing, like a tweed sandwich, or a double-decker one. I enjoy combining multiple tweedy elements for greater complexity in my finished yarn and cloth.

Always sample before committing to the entire carding and spinning process. Be sure to let the sample roll rest and expand for a few minutes to see the true flecking results.

Tweeds vs. Heathers

Visually, tweeds and heathers are related and may even intersect. Historically, a true tweed fabric begins with a fully carded wool that's then spun with a woolen draw. This helps the nubby bits adhere to the airy wool, aiding in the weather-proofing of the woven yarn and cloth. Tweed is also a visual style inspiration, as the look and feel of the complex, slubby end cloth is sophisticated and classic in the fashion and textiles industries. A heathered yarn has a similar look in terms of color complexity, only it's made by combining two or more different colors (shades, hues, etc.) together as the background colors, pre-spinning. These may be natural wool colors or dyed, and blending them together prior to spinning creates a visual soften-ing of the colors in the end fabric, which may also appear flecked and/or contain tweeded bits.

Figures 3.17 and 3.18 Light-as-air, tweedy rolags carded from a medium (dyed) fleece, dyed com-mercial top, silks, and Angelina.

Figure 3.19 Heathering and tweed combine in this handspun yarn and knit sample.

Figure 3.20 These puni-rolags were carded with a more heathered than textural effect in mind.

Figures 3.21 and 3.22 A fully heathered effect, using layered scrap fiber.

Stripes/Repeating Colors

I consider this to be one of the best-known uses of rolags and roll-ups and a non-fussy means of color management. Just lay your fibers down in vertical columns and repeating color order. For longer color repeats, lay wider stripes. For shorter runs, lay down narrower ones. Or, go wild with a more casual, heathery striping, such as in the scraptastic rolag in figures 3.23 and 3.24.

Figures 3.23 and 3.24 Random, scrappy stripes make interesting roll-ups and yarns.

To make sure your colors are the main effect, tamp them down into the cloth with your fat paintbrush or tamping brush before carding the entire board at once. This ensures your color play is the star of your spin and that you don't end up with a fully heathered roll-up and yarn. Be sure to build up your layers as precisely as possbile, *without leaving any gapping between your stripes.* Otherwise, you'll have visibly weakened areas where the stripes connect.

You may also use texture or other visual effects in one or more of your striping columns to create a different type of striping.

Figure 3.25 These roll-ups include a lovely sparkle repeat, while the ones in figures 3.26, 3.27, and 3.28 take texture to another level, including the use of sanitized, backyard feathers.[14]

14 To sanitize feathers, I first freeze them in a plastic bag, inside the deep freezer, for at least three days (to kill any parasites). I then soak them in a sudsy mix of warm water and dish soap for 30 minutes, being sure to gently remove any dirt with my gloved fingers. Finally, I soak them in a solution of 50/50 rubbing alcohol and hydrogen peroxide for another 30–60 minutes. Rinse and let them dry on a paper towel.

Figures 3.26, 3.27, and 3.28 Stripes with interesting add-ins, such as feathers, will create unique rolags.

Color Blocking

Color blocking can also be a means of repeating colors or patterns, but not always. Here, bold colors or complementary colors appear next to each other, with sharp delineation between them. Blocks of color may be spun in repeating order, like stripes, though striping can also be more muted or disseminated into its finished patterning. There's one key obstacle to color blocking your roll-ups: Spinning from the end of any cylindrical fiber tube will diffuse the contrast. To get around this, you'll want to keep the beginning and ending edges of your rolags from sealing together when you roll them from the blending board. When you're ready to spin, you can then unroll the tube(s) and split the fiber down vertically and spin each color individually, or however else you choose. Be sure to tamp down your fibers fully prior to carding them, to minimize heathering of the edges.

Want another option? Just card each color separately, then spin these roll-offs in your desired striping/color or pattern-repeating order. Experiment with using different sized roll-offs in the same spin, for added impact.

Figure 3.30 This spin is based on same-sized deep brown repeats, interspersed with shorter runs of blended jewel colored roly-polies.

Gradients

A gradient differs from a color block in that there's a notable blending or overlap of colors, creating a new, transitional color or colors. The main colors need not be related, and you may use whatever color progression you'd like. There are multiple ways to prepare a gradient spin with your roll-ups, including these.

Vertical and Horizontal Gradients

These gradients are made by laying down blocks of overlapping color either vertically or horizontally, creating shifting, intermediate colors either across or up the carding cloth. Burnish well as you layer for the smoothest intermediary changes, then roll as desired for a gradient spin (figures 3.31, 3.32, and 3.33). Laying your colors in a standard formation across the board produces runs of shifting color when rolled off and spun from the end, while stacking the colors vertically yields a completely different effect, allowing the user to roll off each color (including the new transitional

Figure 3.29 Color blocking.

colors) individually. Laying down three colors, you will be able to roll off four or five individual colors in your gradient sequence. Layer lightly and burnish often for the most blended effect. You can also make a set of rolags/puni-rolags and spin them back-to-back for a repeating gradient (figures 3.34, 3.35, and 3.36).

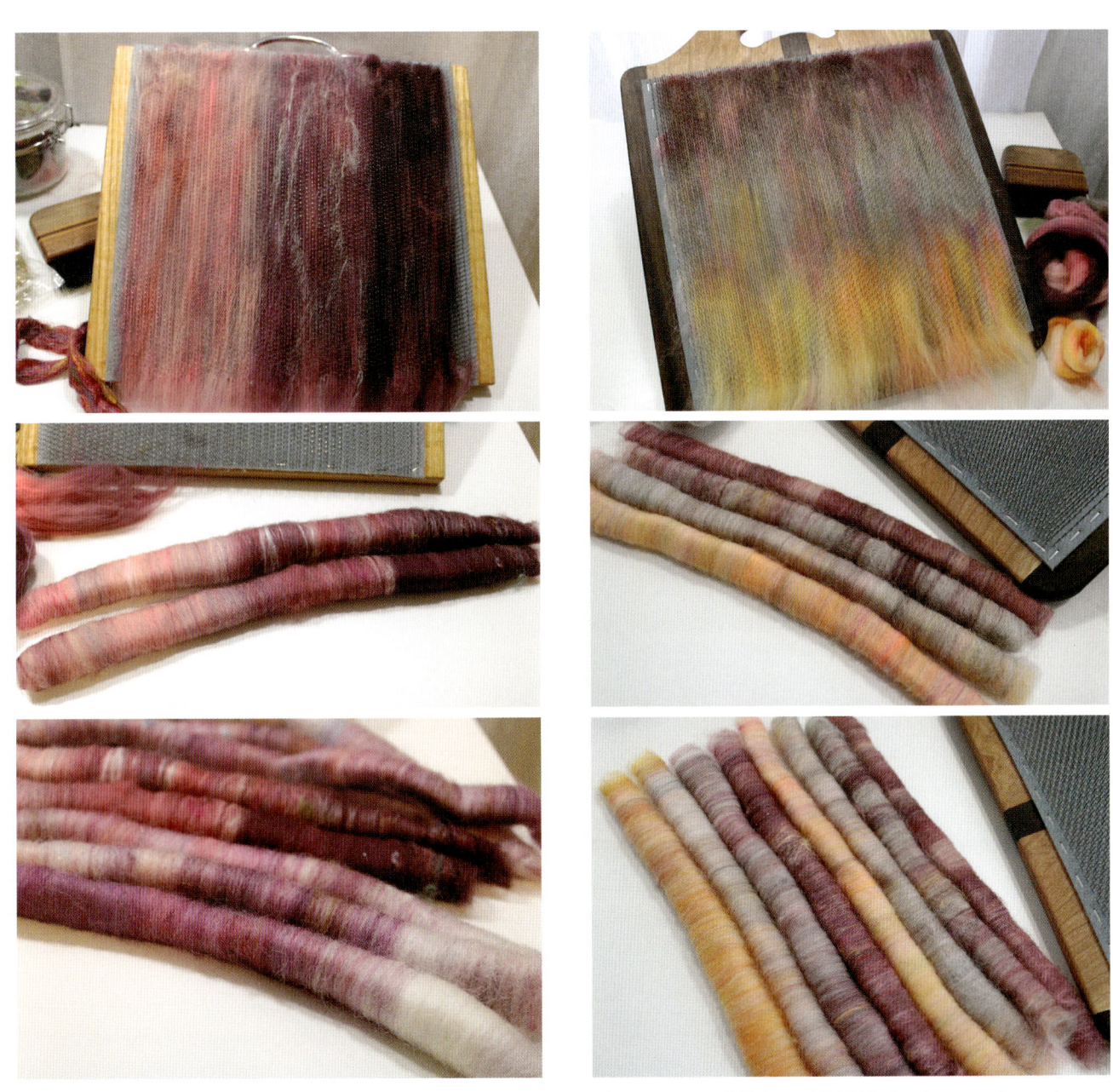

Figures 3.31, 3.32, and 3.33 Place gradient colors in order across the board, overlapping to create intermediate colors, burnishing well. Roll off as desired.

Figures 3.34, 3.35, and 3.36 Spin these roll-ups back-to-back for a repeating gradient effect. The smaller/narrower the roll-ups, the shorter the repeats will be in your yarn.

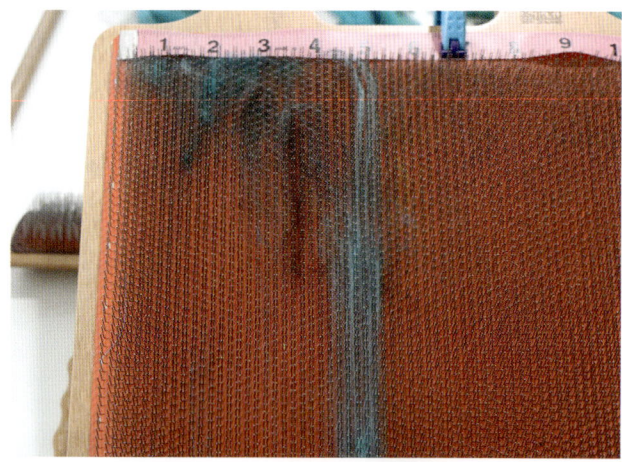

Figures 3.37, 3.38, and 3.39 This subtle gradient set is made up of a blue-green base color and black, to deepen the base color's shade, and a smidge of carding waste for extra interest. Note the use of the clipped-on measuring tape, so I can easily judge the length of my roly-polies for continuity.

Individually Carded Gradients

Don't be afraid of this straightforward, simple math, which can be done in your head. Results can be astonishing. Working with just two base colors is a good way to practice your introduction to this model, where each make of the blending board is its own segment within the final gradient. Each end rolag/roll-up should weigh as close to the same amount as possible. You can take the process as far as you'd like numerically. If you'd prefer to work with tone, tint, or shade instead of mixing hues, add gray, white, or black, respectively, to a single starting color, and blend together in progressively increasing amounts, using the same theory.

You'll also need your scale to weigh out your starting amounts. In this instance, I like to work with grams because I am better able to tabulate small but incremental amounts for my blending process. Here, my goal is a 50-gram, five-color shaded gradient, with each separate segment weighing 10 grams. I've got my cloth tape measure clamped to the top of my blending board to help keep my extra-fat roly-polies the same size on the board, and I lay down a light outline as an added visual aid when filling the space.

My first squat roll-off is 90 percent my base color (blue-green) plus 10 percent black. My second is 80 percent blue-green plus 20 percent black, and so on, so my fifth roly-poly is a 50/50 blend, but this particular formula would make a lovely seven-roll-up gradient, too, ending with a 25/75 base/black blend, were I to continue the progression. These smaller roll-ups make for excellent sampling of project ideas.

See how simple? This scalable progression means that you can spin for any amount needed with assurance by carding up multiple makes of each segment. You can also come back to card more fiber if needed, without worrying about the new lot being a match to the first. Work in percentage increments that make sense to you and the amount of fiber needed for your project. For the most thorough color blending, be sure to lay both colors in light, wispy staple lengths. I also find that holding my two colors together in my hand as I work assists in better integration of the fibers (figure 3.40).

Figure 3.40 Holding two colors in my hand as I work ensures better integration of the fibers.

Figures 3.41 and 3.42 First pass vs. second pass. The difference in the two is notable.

I utilized a double-carding technique, normally used in drum carding, to further blend the black and green fibers together, proving that indeed, one can absolutely blend color and materials on the blending board just as well as one can using a drum carder or hand cards (figure 3.42).

To double-card your baby batt strip, grip it firmly and lift the batt up and off the carding cloth (figure 3.43). Strip it down into smaller lengths, making sure to turn each section inside out or however needed to expose any incongruous, chunkier areas in need of more thorough carding (figure 3.44). You can repeat this process one more time, for a total of three passes (if desired), without damaging your fiber or creating neps. Roll the fully blended fiber off the board, and move onto your next color segment.

Figure 3.43 To double-card your baby batt strip, grip it firmly and lift the batt up and off the carding cloth.

Figure 3.44 Strip the once-carded batt down into smaller lengths, making sure to turn each section inside out or however needed to expose any incongruous, chunkier areas in need of more thorough carding, and then reload and card another time.

Variegates/Checkerboard

"Variegated" yarn can be many things, but at its heart it's a multicolored yarn that's dipped, painted, or otherwise hand-dyed so each color has its own evenly spaced, repeating increments when put to use. They're wildly appealing to most knitters, crocheters, and weavers. This same effect may be created with your blending board, with any size roll-up. My favorite way to do this is by creating a repeating checkerboard pattern with my rolls (figure 3.45), though the same premise holds with any kind of pattern repeat that appeals to you. Spin your rolags in "checkerboard" order, creating a unique but repeating space-dyed-like impact in your finished yarn.

Figure 3.45 To make the checkerboard rolags, I carded two inverse color repeats on my blending board and rolled off these puni-style rolags, arranging them as you see here. Spinning them in this order will yield a strand of variegated yarn.

Fractals

Fractals are a means of color management stemming from the mathematical theory of fractals and complex wholes,[15] where a whole pattern self-repeats infinitely on a smaller and smaller scale. (Think: a boldly painted length of fiber and how breaking it down lengthwise into narrower strips creates shorter runs of the same color pattern.)[16]

---

15 https://en.wikipedia.org/wiki/Fractal.

16 Janel Laidman, *Spin Off* magazine, 2007.

Your "whole" serves as one ply of your spin, while your smaller self-repeats are spun one after the other and become your second ply. This can also be taken further by creating even smaller self-repeats as your third ply, and so on. Sure, this is more of a "fractal-light" vs. a true, decreasing-scale self-repeat, but that's okay. Roly-polies are the perfect application for fractals, but other bigger/smaller color and/or patterning repeats could come in the form of one rolog (rolled log) combined with a few rolags or puni-rolags. If you happen to have two blending boards, try loading them at the same time for more accurate scalability, but if not, just reload your blending board and roll smaller units on the second make.

Here are two examples to get you thinking up your own fractal-ish ideas.

Method 1: Start off with an easily repeatable color pattern, such as stripes or color blocks, so that your second make of the board is as close to identical to the first as possible. Roll the first set of roll-ups as one large rolled log, or a set of rolags, puni-style rolags, etc. Roll the second round into smaller roll-ups, such as the punis shown beneath the thicker puni-rolags in figure 3.46.

Figure 3.46 For fractals, roll the first set of roll-ups as one large rolled log or a set of rolags. Roll the second round into smaller roll-ups, such as the punis shown here beneath the thicker puni-rolags

Method 2: Create a pattern that's easily split into larger and smaller repeats from a single make of the board, then split the burnished fiber and roll it off into larger and smaller pattern-repeating roll-ups (figures 3.47 to 3.51).

Figures 3.47, 3.48, 3.49, 3.50, and 3.51 Method 2 for making fractals.

4

BATTS AND CLOUDS, ROVINGS AND SLIVERS

Most of us (erroneously) believe that "real" batts can only be made on a drum carder. While acquiring a well-made drum carder is indeed an achievement, it's not a realistic one for everyone. My blending board batts and rovings are 100 percent indistinguishable from those made on my drum carder, and yours can be too! Can you tell which batts and rovings were made on a drum carder and which were made on a blending board in these photos?

The drum carder was built with the at-home spinner in mind, in a time when spinners mainly had access to sheared fleeces and a minimal breed selection of milled top. Our industry and associated hobbies have expanded along with the age of technology, allowing handspinners to share not only access to supplies, but our creative ideas, endeavors, and discoveries. Beyond batts and various rovings, the blending board is capable of re-creating, or serving as a step in creating, every carded fiber preparation in this chapter.

Now, who needs a drum carder? Not you!

Figure 4.1 Can you tell which is which? A set of each of these rolled logs and rovings were carded on a coarse-cloth, vintage Pat Green drum carder and a set carded on my coarse (48 PPI) blending board. Even I cannot tell them apart without their identifying tags.

BATTS

A batt is a square or rectangular pillow of fiber that's been carded open using a drum carder, hand cards, or a blending board with a blending brush, just the same as described and used in chapter 3's roll-offs. The difference here is, instead of rolling off, the carded fiber is removed whole from the blending board. Unlike a rolag or its counterparts, a batt may be broken down and spun in innumerable ways, providing the spinner with more options in attaining their intended yarn, or simply with more woolen to worsted-like outcomes through the combination of fiber play, spinning draw, and preparation experimentation. You can spin directly from a batt (a tad cumbersome), break off chunks and spin them in color order or randomly, tear your batt into equal or random-sized strips, attenuate it into a continuous roving, diz a roving, and so much more. Your approach to batt making is the basis for every additional preparation in this chapter.

Better Batts

Carded batts are an absolute joy to behold and to spin, and I've yet to meet the spinner who wasn't in some way drawn to their lush beauty. A cushiony batt feels ripe with possibilities and may be used to spin anything from a lively cobweb lace to an airy lopi singles to core-spun yarn, 3-ply sweater yarn, cabled and crepe yarns, and more. Batts are also more easily adaptable to spinning a wider range of gauges than a rolag or other rolled preparation, as the maximum girth of a spun singles tends to be limited by the diameter of the roll-up used to spin it. A batt's airiness brings a unique life to the yarns made with it, no matter the technique employed in the spinning. Batts are adaptable to wool and other protein fibers of varying lengths and traits—even longer wools and coarser fibers—and carding them is made that much easier thanks to the blending board's flat surface. You may choose to build a batt that's chock-full of chunky texture or one that's perfectly smooth, or one anywhere along the way. Color play and textural applications are infinite.

A "typically carded" batt is indeed light and lofty, but the fibers are still somewhat aligned by the tines on the carding cloth. As with our rolled preparations in chapter 3, your technical approach can help you lean further into the woolen process—and even attain it—by directionally

A.

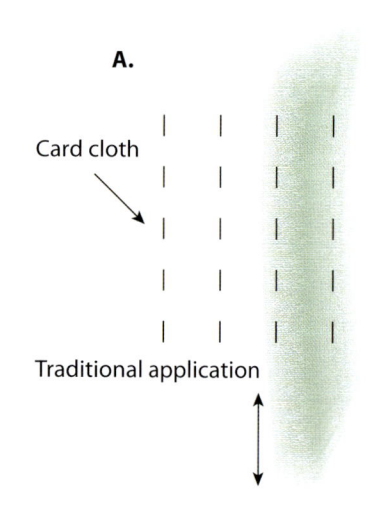

Card cloth

Figure 4.2 Fiber can be loaded onto the blending board in a typical vertical fashion or multidirectionally for more woolen-ness.

Traditional application

B.

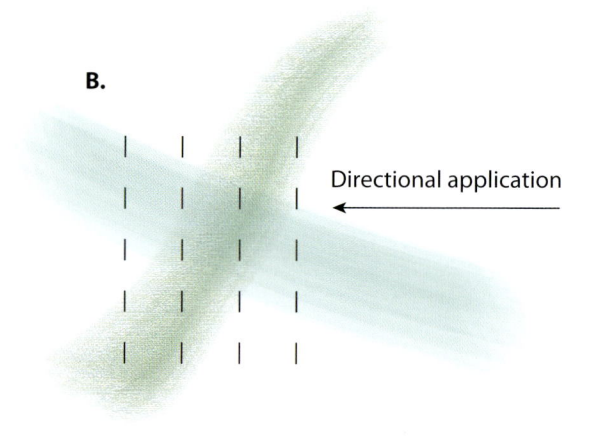

Directional application

loading your fiber onto your blending board, while color applications such as striping, gradients, and even thorough, full blending, are achievable by using multiple carding passes on the board, similar to when using a drum carder or hand cards.

As with any carded preparation, your choice in fiber matters. You may use any breed of wool and/or other protein fiber as your base, though I find that including wool in my blends helps them to hold together in their batt and related formats. Combed top is a wonderful choice, as is cleaned fleece, which, as always, must be picked or teased open for best results. Combining top with fleece or locks makes for wonderfully complex and wooly batts. Currently, I'm enamored of using assorted hand-dyed locks, from ultra-fine Rambouillet to long and wavy Corriedale, in my batts. Even long and silky Teeswater has its place on the blending board. Depending on the length of the fiber and its traits, I may card the locks open fully; other times, such as when working with superlong, shiny locks, I tamp them into place as colorful elements to enjoy in textured art yarn spinning.

A little-known benefit of using a blending board to card your batts: Your choice in blending brush acts similarly to the licker-in of a drum carder, in that it helps to hold the fiber strands extended so they catch against the tines while burnishing. Unlike when working with two drums, however, there's less likelihood of your fiber bouncing back and snapping on itself, creating neps from over-extension.

No matter your choice in fiber or combination, the preparations in this chapter rely on one opposite of the rolled preparations in the last chapter, and that's in the amount of fiber used. To help your batts and rovings maintain their shape and structure, *pack your board full*. Other best practices remain the same.

Make the Best Batts

Make sure your fiber source is picked/teased open (fleece) or fully decompacted (combed top) through a good "tease and whip." The same goes for any textural inclusions. Use scissors to snip small pieces/lengths, so each plane of its surface can be well burnished for better blending (and thus better adhesion during spinning). When using recycled materials such as denim, fabric, ribbon, or novelty yarn, break or strip the material down to its threads or smallest elements, again to help bond the materials. ***Note:*** If your style choice is a chunkier one, that's okay too. You can leave these inclusions as they are. Just be aware that chunky mix-ins are harder to fully card into your fiber since they won't adhere as well, though you can address this during the spinning and plying processes, at least to some effect.

Be sure to build an overhang at the base of your blending board. This sheaf of fiber is your stabilization point for removing your batt and dizzing your roving (see page 82).

Layer Your Fiber in Thin Staple Lengths, Burnishing Often

When adding texture and/or any type of inclusions, thin strands yield the best adhesion to the batt and the spun singles, although partially picked elements and bolder inclusions can make for unique yarn designs.

Remove the Batt from the Blending Board

Removing your batt in its whole form couldn't be simpler. Using both hands and starting at the outer edges, loosen the bottom overhang, snapping it firmly upward to release it from the teeth beneath, reducing the chances of leaving stray strands behind. The end goal is to pick up the batt as one continuous unit using either your hands or a pair of dowels. Either continue pulling the batt firmly upward by hand (figure 4.3) or use the dowels to clasp the loosened base and roll the batt up loosely (figures 4.4 and 4.5), without locking it closed. *Do not attenuate as you roll.* If any fibers do get left behind, stop and brush (or pick) them up onto the underside of the batt as needed. Gently unroll your batt and let it breathe and expand. The more air you card into your layers, the greater the potential expansion amount (figures 4.6 and 4.7).

Figure 4.3 Pick up the batt in one continuous motion by pulling upward firmly.

Figures 4.4 and 4.5 Dowels can be used to clasp and roll the batt upward.

Figures 4.6 and 4.7 The more air you card into your layers, the greater the potential expansion amount.

My blending board batts weigh in at approximately 1.5 to 1.75 ounces of fiber depending on my fiber choices and which board and card cloth I'm using. It's easy to tell when the board is full by checking the side view of the tines. Your smoothed fibers will create an even surface just above, or right at, the tops of the carding teeth. Batts are more forgiving visually than rolled preparations, as any sparser areas, if present, won't show through—*though these areas will appear as thinner bands if the batt is then pulled into a roving.* These batts weigh about the same amount as my comparably made, standard-sized, drum-carded batts.

Make It a Double

To make a fuller, 2-plus ounce or greater sized batt, simply make two of the same (or contrasting, complementary, or whatever color and textural composition pleases you) batts and remove them from the blending board. Lay them next to each other with two raw edges touching. Use a blending brush to lightly seam the edges together, being careful not to damage the fibers in the process (figures 4.8 to 4.11).

Make It More Woolen with Multiple and Directional Passes

The process of carding a standard, at-home batt results in a lush and lofty pillow of somewhat aligned fiber with woolen characteristics. However, more directional—or even haphazard—placement of your fibers will produce a more woolen, or fully woolen, preparation respectively, ready to trap even more air in your spinning.

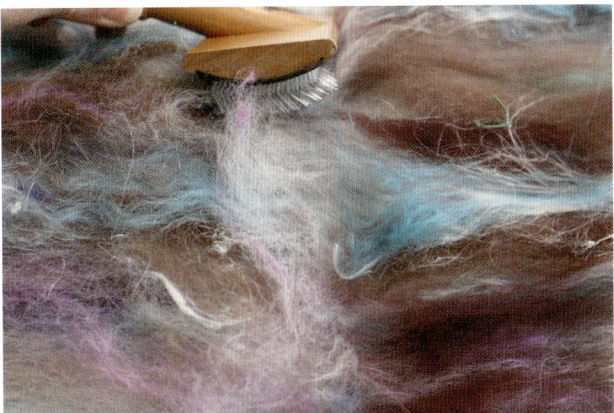

Figures 4.8, 4.9, 4.10, and 4.11 To create a larger batt, gently seam together two raw edges of the same (or complementary) batts using your blending brush.

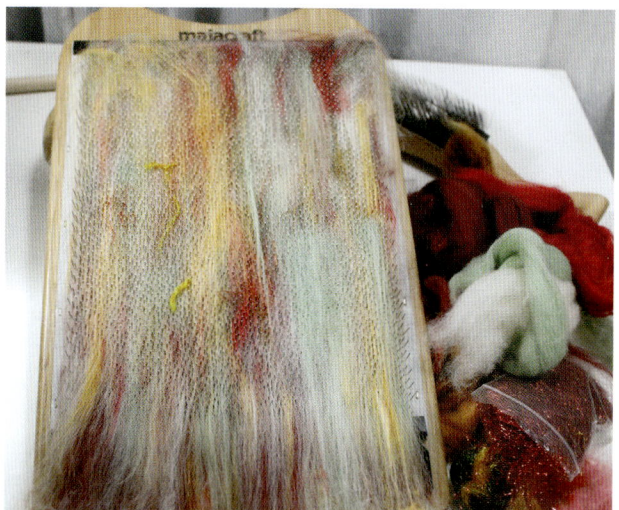

Figures 4.12, 4.13, and 4.14 These batts (top) were made with the same medium-staple commercial top, longer shinies, and blending board, but the one on the left was created with typical vertical staple placement and the one on the right was made with diagonal and randomized placement. Note how much more air is carded into the batt on the right.

Directional Loading

Just as discussed in chapters 2 and 3, directional loading of your blending board can ensure a more dissimilar arrangement of your fiber strands for a more woolen-like preparation and spin. You could employ a thoughtful placement of horizontal and vertical layering, diagonal layering, or any combination, though more haphazard placement and/or cross placement may be more your speed (it's certainly mine). For a fully woolen effect in your fiber prep, let loose and card up a cloud, which is made from completely arbitrary placement of multilength fibers. Adding multiple passes to your process will help you not only in more thorough and complete color and textural blending, but also in building the airiest of batts.

Per usual, selecting denser and bouncier fibers will yield a fuzzier finish not only to your carded fiber preparation, but also to your spun yarn.

Figure 4.15 The middle and top batts in this stack were made using commercial top, while the bottom batt is carded from a mix of fine- to medium-staple dyed fleece and traps more air in its layers.

Recard Your Batt

I'm embarrassed to say how many years it took me to figure out that a batt could be reloaded and burnished a second (and third!) time on the blending board, using the same "second pass" technique one would apply to drum carding. This is useful in a range of situations, including when I'm working with an especially dense and short fleece that doesn't blend as smoothly as I'd like on the first pass, and with coarser wools that I'd like to blend with slicker fiber such as silks or mohair, and with tougher-to-blend fibers including alpaca, musk ox, and possum, which can be difficult to thoroughly/invisibly blend into wool due to differences in follicle structure and makeup. Multiple passes are also useful for fully blending colors (as seen in chapter 3) and mix-ins like tweeds or other small inclusions. Simply remove your blended batt, split it down into smaller strips or sections, and reload your blending board using one piece at a time, burnishing again as you go. (Depending on your fiber, it will be well fluffed at this point and take up far more space, so here you can get away with laying down thicker layers than you would normally.) Be sure to coax open the carded strips to fully blend from the inside out if you're seeking a thorough blending.

Figures 4.16 and 4.17 Hand-dyed CVM x Merino cross, alpaca fleece, backyard Shetland locks, scraps of top, dyed fine to medium locks, Angelina, eri and other silks, firestar, hand-dyed top, and plain medium-staple top.

Figures 4.18 and 4.19 Single- and double-carded batt. Note how the colors are more subtle and fibers more blended after a second carding pass.

Make It More Worsted

To spin a smoother, more compressed batt, work with longer fibers with smoother cuticles, being sure to lay them down vertically. Processed shinies, including silks, nylon, firestar, bamboo, and Tencel, make an excellent addition. Lay the fiber down in long, open strips and *tamp* it into place using your soft-bristled tamping or packing brush, then card.

Remove the batt from the board and spin the fiber with your focus on keeping the strands smooth and compressed, without letting them twist in between your hands as you draft out your singles, and/or pull them further into a parallel alignment before beginning (see "Roving Preparations" on page 76).

No matter the directionality of the fibers, batts are the basis for hand-pulling and dizzing rovings of various ranges of fluffiness and smoothness.

Figures 4.20, 4.21, and 4.22 For a smoother, more worsted-like batt, lay your fiber in strips and tamp down the fiber instead of carding it. Use silken and/ or longer-stapled fibers.

CARDED CLOUDS

Make It the Most Woolen

Cloud preparation is probably the least known of all commercial/milled preparations. It's a 100 percent woolen preparation where teased- or picked-open fibers are laid in random directions before going through the carder, with short/uneven bits included in the mix. The result is a puff of opened, cloud-like fiber, with strands jumbled in all directions. It may be spun many ways, and the resulting yarn is typically imperfect but unusually airy.

To create a fully woolen, carded cloud, use clean, picked-open fleece or a combination of teased locks and top or roving, and build light, randomly placed layers with plenty of burnishing along the way. Feel free to add a little Angelina, if it hits, or other colorful ingredients. Or, let the simple beauty of your wool do all the talking.

You'll get a woolen-ish (but not fully woolen) result from using commercial fiber instead of locks, especially if you card together tops made from different, dissimilar breeds and lengths, blends, or ingredients. Using a single type of top on its own is a fun way to better understand carded clouds, though the results will be far less woolen and not a true cloud.

Figures 4.23, 4.24, 4.25, 4.26, 4.27, and 4.28 Card up a cloud with fibers of dissimilar lengths, placed and burnished haphazardly, such as the dyed Romney locks and undyed silver angora shown here.

ROVING VS. SLIVER

The terms "roving" and "combed top" are often used interchangeably, but they are different fiber preparations. Combed top is technically *not* roving. A true combed top is just that: fleece/locks, with all tips facing the same direction, processed using hand combs. This removes any unequal lengths and leaves the fiber in alignment. The fiber may then be dizzed into a fully worsted, more compressed sliver,[17] directly from one of the combs. This is the only true, 100 percent worsted preparation. Commercial, or milled, top is processed fiber that's also had its shorter strands removed through machine combing, leaving equal-sized staple lengths behind. These are then organized and compressed into sheaves made of parallel staple lengths, but the processing leaves a less perfect result than that obtained by hand-combing. This is what's most commonly sold online and by independent (and commercial) dyers and resellers, despite the often-erroneous label, as "roving." Roving always starts out carded. It's mostly aligned, with cross-directional areas, making a delightfully fluffy, long rope of fiber that's usually a nice thick width. Roving is made commercially or by hand. A hand-made roving can be made any number of ways, and just as with commercial roving, you'll note a slight natural twist to it. A batt makes an excellent starting point for pulling a roving. A carded roving is still fluffy, puffy, and light, and you can manipulate its woolen-ness through both directional blending board loading and even direction-based hand-processing of the batt itself.

17   In addition to the noted characteristics, a "rope" of sliver may appear thinner in girth than a roving. It has no natural twist to it, unlike a rope of roving.

Figure 4.29 Carded roving.

Pin-drafted Roving

This is a potential step in mill processing, where the carded roving is pulled through a series of pins, which help to pull and realign the fibers after they've been carded. Since this is a roving, there may be short bits in the fiber, as well as some disorganization of the strands. The fiber is compressed and finished like a milled combed top, creating a commercial fiber that's loftier than plain top. Some spinners find that pulling carded fiber through a diz can produce a similar, at-home result. Dizzing may be done on its own or added as a finishing step to prepared fiber, both on and off the blending board.

Figure 4.30 Both strips of fiber came from the same carded batt. The one on the left was dizzed, further organizing and compressing the staples of fiber within.

Make Your Own Roving, Multiple Ways

Creating your own roving is an absolute blast that never gets old. There are several ways to do so. Which approach is best? That's up to you, though sometimes desired color effects and/or the amount of texture you've included will help point you in the right direction. (Heavily textured fiber will get stuck in most dizzes, for instance.) Take note of how each method yields slightly different traits along the woolen to worsted range as you work your way through these processes.

Hand-pulled Rovings: from a Batt/Cloud or Roll-up, as a Z-strip

From a Batt/Cloud. Hand-pulling a roving from a batt or cloud is simple, and if you've ever pre-drafted commercial top prior to spinning it, you're familiar with the steps: Take a batt and strip it down into smaller, narrower lengths. Then carefully attenuate the strips—ideally, without breaking the staple lengths—from one end to the other. You can work by gently attenuating the fiber toward or against you, whichever feels more comfortable. This draws the fluffed fibers more parallel. Roll the pre-drafted fiber up into a nest to keep it safe and tidy. If you'd like, repeat the process, further aligning the fibers and thinning the roving. (Effects added: The strands of fiber are pulled into more alignment but will still capture some air in the spun yarn.)

This easy technique works with all your carded fibers, from smooth to very chunky. To add even more loft to the pulled roving, layer and card your batt using directional and/or random placement of your fibers first, or stack two batts (or fiber strips) with intentional direction (e.g., with the grains running in the same direction or in two different directions for even greater fluff).

Figure 4.31 Pulled roving is also a good way to work with color and runs of color, including striping, repeats, etc., in your spinning.

Figures 4.32, 4.33, 4.34, 4.35, 4.36, and 4.37 Strip your batt down and gently attenuate the fibers into a continuous roving; repeat the pre-drafting again if a narrower result is desired. Roll the roving into a nest when you've achieved the width of the strip and the alignment you like.

From a Roll-up. This method mimics the one above, using a roll-up as your starting point. Your rolog or puni may be any size or thickness, though its girth helps set the potential parameters of your spun yarn's thickness. Hand-pulling a roving from one large log is a personal favorite—the aeration is unbelievable—while attenuating from a puni or puni-rolag produces a more streamlined result due to the difference in cylindrical size.

To maintain a more aligned directional effect of your staple placement (i.e., for a smoother, more worsted-like effect), remove your batt and roll it up side to side (figure 4.40) instead of the more typical bottom to top (figure 4.41), then pull and/ or diz a roving (figure 4.42).

Figure 4.40 Batt rolled side to side.

Figure 4.41 Batt rolled bottom to top.

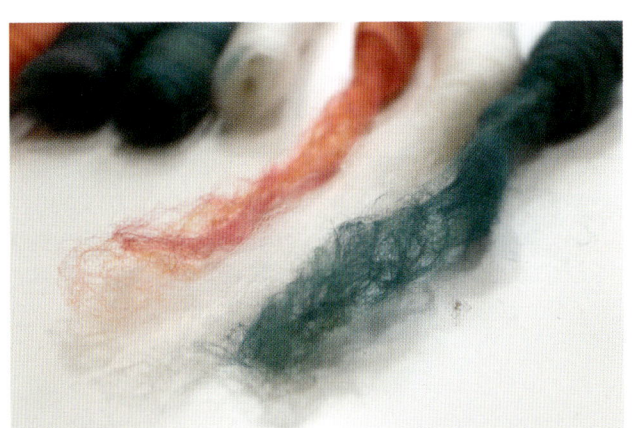

Figures 4.38 and 4.39 Your favorite roll-ups make an excellent base for hand-pulled roving. (Effect added: The fibers will cross more randomly in your spinning, for a boost in loft. If you're working with stripes or color blocks within your individual roll-up(s), the demarcations between colors will soften as you attenuate the tube of fiber.)

Figure 4.42 The roving on the right was dizzed from the side-to-side strip shown in figure 4.40; the one on the left made from the typical, bottom-to-top roll-up shown in figure 4.41 and dizzed from one end, resulting in slightly more air and remaining disorganization.

As a Z-strip. This method makes a continuous roving from a single batt or two stacked batts. The carded fibers are pulled both vertically and horizontally in the Z-stripping process, allowing for areas that are more aligned combined with areas that remain more jumbled. Besides . . . a fluffy roving nest made from an attenuated Z-strip is irresistible. This method works regardless of whether your batt is smooth or textured and provides a means for managing color repeats and striping, working with gradients or achieving other color effects. (Effects added: A bit of everything—some alignment and an added pop of some predictable disorganization, too.)

Step 1: Lay the batt on a flat surface. Starting at one end of the batt and working with the direction of the grain of the fibers (when possible), gently tear a length of fiber either toward (down) or away (up) from you, being sure to stop about an inch from the edge so the batt remains intact.

Step 2: Tear the next length from the opposite direction, still stopping an inch or so before the edge. Tear another strip, exactly as in Step 1, completing one "Z" pattern.

Step 3: Repeats steps 1 and 2 until you've reached the opposite corner of the batt.

Step 4: Gently attenuate the entire strip from end to end to pull a continuous roving of your desired width, then roll it up into a nest. Feel free to add a dizz along the way.

Diz a Roving or Sliver

Dizzes come in different materials, shapes, and sizes, though you likely have household items on hand that could be used, too (see chapter 2, page 25, for more information). Dizzing adds a different element to a roving preparation, acting more like industrial pin aligners used in milled pin-drafted roving, realigning and *sometimes* smoothing down the exterior of the fiber you're preparing. This staple realignment comes from the friction between the diz's snug slot or hole and the fiber being pulled through it combined with the action of attenuating the fibers themselves. A diz may be paired with hand combs to create a fully worsted preparation, known as a sliver, though it may also be added to a carded preparation to diz a roving. It's equally useful whether your batt is still on the board or off it, to further modify the traits of a roving or a roll-up. I love the added swirling effect it makes with my rovings, too, creating especially inviting nests of colorfully blended fibers and mix-ins (figure 4.43). A dizzed roving still has fabulous fluff—just with a slightly more orderly and compressed fiber arrangement—for when you want to help highlight a denser or smoother fiber and/or yarn. Confident, continuous dizzing takes practice, so give yourself permission to keep trying, if at first you don't succeed.

Smooth, semi-smooth, and lightly textured fiber blends are optimal with a diz, as those made from highly textural ingredients tend to get stuck in the small holes/slots of the tool during the dizzing process.

Figure 4.44 Roving dizzed from puni-rolags.

Figure 4.43 I love the added swirling effect a diz makes with my rovings, creating especially inviting nests of colorfully blended fibers and mix-ins.

You may have items around the house that could serve as starter dizzes (buttons, metal washers, etc.), but one that's lightweight and concave is easiest to use. Holding it with the hollow side facing upward toward the fiber source makes a smoother surface finish (figure 4.45 and right side roving in figure 4.46), while holding it opposite, with the concavity toward you (left in figure 4.46), creates more friction against the fiber and leaves a fuzzier outer surface.

Figure 4.45 This roving was first attenuated in figures 4.33 to 4.35 and then dizzed here. The outside of the roving is more smooth when you hold the diz with the hollow side facing toward the fiber source.

Figure 4.46 Holding the diz with the concavity toward you (shown left) will create more friction and leave a fuzzier outside surface.

Diz from the Board

This method is worked side to side in rows, up from the bottom of the board, and starts from either corner of the overhang. Beginners tend to use both hands while learning to diz a roving from the blending board . . . one holds and moves the button or diz, pushing it up to the backs (the knees) of the carding teeth and guiding it in the proper direction, while the other pinches the threaded fiber, drafting it firmly through the hole, staple length by staple length and keeping the supply taut and unbroken. The guiding hand gently moves the diz across the rows with the "pushing" motion while the "pinch-and-pull" hand draws the next staple length and attenuates it downward. With a good diz and some practice, you'll be dizzing one-handed before you know it, freeing up the other hand to hold the carded fiber down against the tines for greater combing/alignment result (see figure 4.49 on page 84).

Either way, this method of dizzing is a rhythmic, "pull, push, pull, push, pull . . . " waltz across and up your blending board.

Step 1: Thread a few strands from one bottom corner of the overhang through your diz.

To make threading the diz easier, twist several strands of fiber together at one corner of your overhang, and pull them through the diz using your fingers, a tiny crochet hook, or threader.

Using your "fiber supply" hand (the hand you keep further from your wheel when spinning), hold the diz up against the knee backs of your carding teeth, pinching the threaded fiber taut with your other hand. Pull a staple length through, just until you feel and see the fiber supply begin to thin, then pinch and hold this amount, tensioned in place. Push the diz, guiding it in the proper direction (in this case, to the left), allowing it to pick up the next strands of fiber for pulling into the roving. Remember to keep the diz on the same level as the teeth, not higher, and angled toward them.

Step 2: Continue the same "push, pull, push, pull" motions as you guide your diz across the row. Your goal is an evenly attenuated strip of fiber.

Step 3: At the end of each row, move up a level and continue in the opposite direction until all the fiber has been removed from the cloth.

Figures 4.47 and 4.48 Roving dizzed from carded Merino top, camel down, cashmere, mulberry and tussah silks, and Angelina.

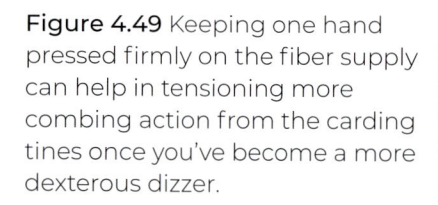

Figure 4.49 Keeping one hand pressed firmly on the fiber supply can help in tensioning more combing action from the carding tines once you've become a more dexterous dizzer.

Off the Batt or Roving

A diz may also be used to further attenuate and organize fiber direction from any format—batt/cloud, roving, top, and even roll-up—once that fiber has been removed from the carding cloth.

Figure 4.50 Textured roving dizzed from the end of a rolled log made from dyed fine fleece.

Double-diz

Diz it twice—using the same diz or two descending-sized holes—to thin your roving into a narrower, even more aligned, strip.

Figure 4.51 Diz your fiber twice for further compression/staple alignment.

Make It More Worsted

Remove your batt from the blending board and roll it up from side to side (vs. bottom to top). Dizz it in this direction or hand-pull the roving more parallel first, before dizzing (see figures 4.40 and 4.42 on page 79).

Lean into the combing capacity of the card cloth. As mentioned, keeping one hand on the board as I attenuate through the diz helps to keep the fibers closer to the tines while I work, allowing the pins to act in a more "comb-like" manner (see figure 4.53). To lean into this more worsted effect, make sure to keep the fiber as close to the tines as possible throughout the process and use longer-stapled, more silken fibers to further enhance worsted elements.

Diz in vertical sections instead of working horizontally by row. Additionally, dizzing in vertical sections (instead of working horizontally) engages the pins of the carding cloth in a singular combing direction, maximizing their impact. As you can see in figures 4.52 to 4.58, I also kept one[18] hand on top of the fiber supply as I pulled/attenuated the staple lengths through the diz with the other, and I used a commercially dyed and processed long-stapled Corriedale top for my main fiber choice. These choices helped me blend my fibers for the smoother, more worsted intent of this spin.

As always, your choice of fiber matters too, as does your manner of laying it down on the blending board.

---

18 I am an ambidextrous spinner. If you're having trouble dizzing your fiber, try swapping hands to see if that's more comfortable.

Figures 4.52, 4.53, 4.54, 4.55, 4.56, 4.57, and 4.58
Dizzing in vertical sections engages the pins of the carding cloth in a singular combing direction, maximizing their impact.

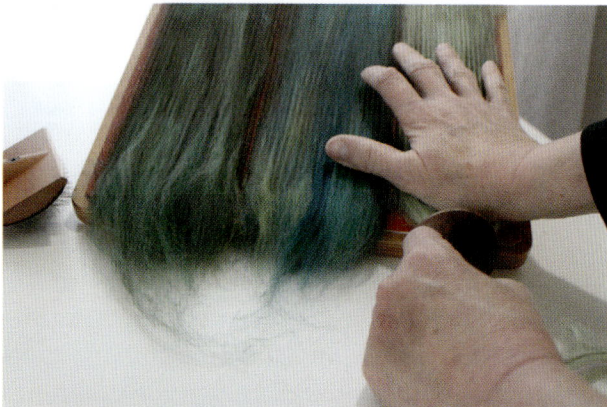

CREATIVE PLAY WITH COLOR AND TEXTURE

Batts, rovings, and the like offer an endless opportunity for color and textural play, and for fun experimentation. Any of the applications utilized in chapter 3 for roll-ups may be reimagined for batts and rovings, too. I especially enjoy repurposing my random fiber scraps into an enticingly fluffy, one-of-a-kind carded batt or roving (figures 4.59, 4.60, and 4.61).

Figures 4.59, 4.60, and 4.61 Random fiber scraps can become a beautiful, fluffy, unique batt or roving.

Flecks/Tweeds and Heathers[19]

Add small flecks of fiber, leftover snips of yarn (airy, woolen yarns will adhere best), silks and noil, silk or banana threads, etc., to your batt for a more dimensional effect. For a heathered background result, thinly layer more than one background color, burnishing often. You can turn a heathered result into a tweeded/flecked one with the addition of noils, garneted waste, or other materials in any color for visual and/or nubby accents in the spun yarn. Be sure to keep your added blips of color or texture light if you plan on using a diz to create a roving.

Figures 4.62 and 4.63 Batts can be made tweedy or heathered with inclusions and/or thin layers of color.

19 See chapter 3 for more thorough term descriptions.

Garneting for Extra Texture

A carded batt makes an ideal setting for working texture into your spinning, no matter how light- or heavy-handed your standard may be.

Excess fabric and denim, ribbon, novelty yarn, and other similar materials will work—all the better if you use a coarser card cloth (figures 4.64, 4.65, and 4.66). Make sure to cut your scraps down into smaller strips prior to taking them to the board, so the carding pins can break down and release the weave of the fabric into threads.

Figures 4.64, 4.65, and 4.66 Garnet (break down) denim and other fabrics, ribbon, and similar materials by snipping them into small pieces to card into your batts.

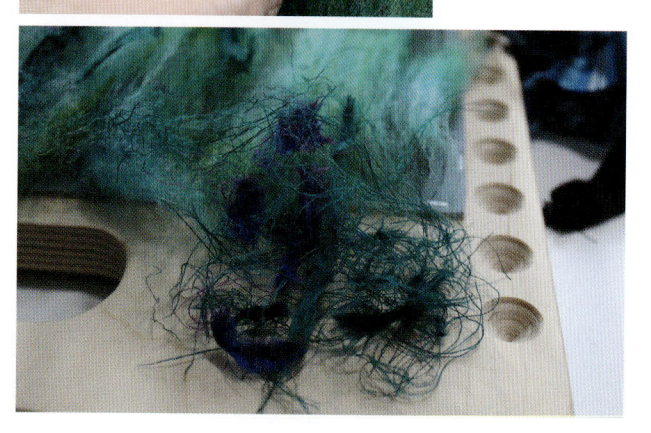

I like to lay a touch of my main fiber onto the board as a light bottom layer, pre-carding, but it's not always necessary to do so (figures 4.67 to 4.72).

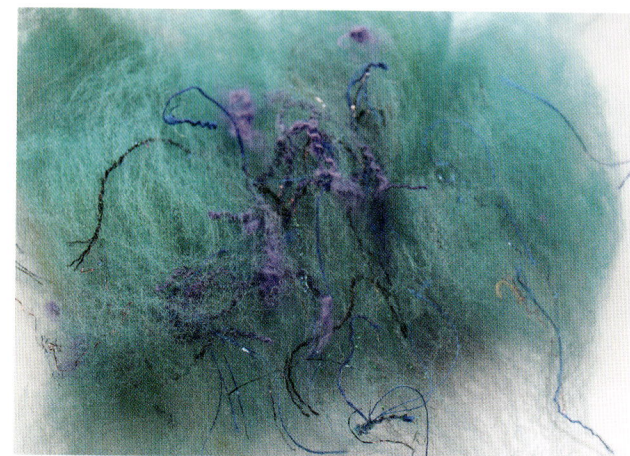

Make It a Marl by Stacking Your Batts

Stacking two batts prior to pulling or dizzing a roving with any of the above techniques offers a creative way to process your own marled fiber blends for spinning. The options are endless, from fiber choice/combinations to color/textural pairings. Further, layering your batts with intentional grain direction, if any, provides yet another facet in planning the woolen characteristics in your project. Stack the batts or roving strips so the grain lies the same way in both batts or, for an even greater woolen effect, so the grain directions are perpendicular, and pull or diz your rovings accordingly. Hand-pulling the layers together leaves the colors lying directly next to each other, while adding a diz afterward (it's more difficult to diz from a batt or roving without attenuating the fibers first) softly swirls the colors together just slightly more cohesively.

Figures 4.73, 4.74, 4.75, 4.76, and 4.77 (continued on page 90) I will often stack two batts, one onto the other, and pull or diz those together into a merged, or marled, roving. The two batts shown here were stacked with the grain of the fibers going in the same direction and then dizzed.

Figures 4.67, 4.68, 4.69, 4.70, 4.71, and 4.72 Lay down a layer of your main fiber and then brush in more fiber and your garneted snippets.

Figures 4.78 and 4.79 Here I used lightly tweeded batts, also stacked with their grain in the same direction.

Stripes/Repeating Colors and Variegates

Lay your colors down in repeating order. If you're hoping to keep the color repeats as crisp as possible, tamp down your bottom layers with your wide paintbrush or packing brush to reduce their crossover and/or build each color separately. Texture or sparkle makes for an excellent addition to one or more color stripes for a more visually complex result. Remove the batt and divide it into its color sections according to your desired outcome, as shown in figures 4.80, 4.81, and 4.82 (spin from a carded strip, a dizzed roving, roving pulled from a roll-up, etc.).

Alternatively, card each color as its own singular batt, remove each from the blending board, then divide them into repeating/striping order for spinning (figures 4.83 and 4.84).

Figure 4.83 You can also card each color individually into its own batt and then divide as desired for striping.

Figure 4.84 Weigh each batt color ingredient before carding and splitting to ensure equal repeats.

Figures 4.80, 4.81, and 4.82 To keep color repeats crisp, divide the colors and remove each batt.

For a variegated yarn effect or stripes/repeats of equal size in your yarn (barring human factors like changes in environment, mood, and other outside factors that impact our spinning), pre-weigh your batt ingredients prior to creating multiple makes of the same repeating patterns (stripes, checkerboards, etc.), and break them down to spin in order.

Figures 4.85 and 4.86 I added a bright yellow dizzed roving to my repeating pattern and weighed out each stripe in my repeat (shown: single repeat).

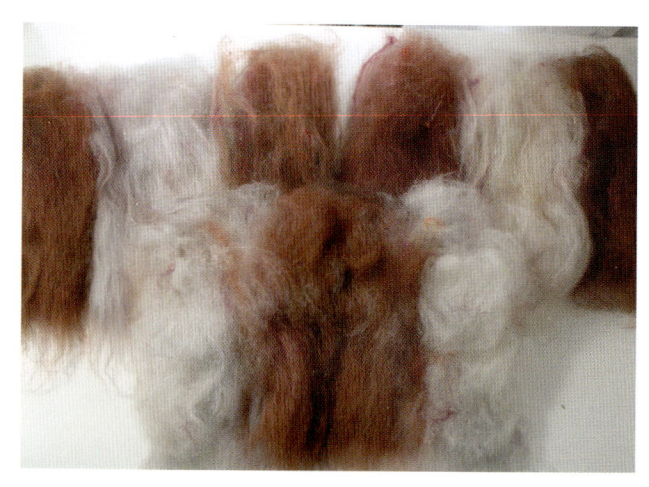

Figure 4.87 Striping/repeating batts in ABA, BAB, ABA order.

Figure 4.88 The ingredients used to make the batts in figure 4.87.

Color Blocking[20]

Since keeping your blocks of color sharp is likely your intention in color blocking, tamping down your first layers instead of carding them will help to minimize their blending crossover (figure 4.89). You can build up each color separately so they never overlap, which makes removing each narrow batt from the blending board that much easier

---

20   See chapter 3 for more information on color blocking.

(figure 4.90). For an even greater woolen effect, roll each color around a dowel to create "fauxlags" once the batt has been removed from the carding cloth (figures 4.91 to 4.92). Repeat the process with multiple makes of the board to turn it into repeating stripes, or dizz two lengths together off the board to spin them as a marl.

Figure 4.89 Tamp down your first layers instead of carding to avoid blending colors.

Figure 4.90 Remove each narrow batt of color separately.

Figures 4.91, 4.92, 4.93, 4.94, and 4.95 Roll each color around a dowel to create "fauxlags."

Figures 4.96, 4.97, 4.98 Spice up an otherwise smooth and moody gradient with a pop of color and unexpected texture, such as these backyard chicken feathers.

Gradients

As mentioned in Chapter 3, a gradient differs from a color block in that the neighboring colors overlap and make their own, in-between, hue. Gradients can run vertically or horizontally (and beyond!). There are many ways to prepare a gradient spin using a batt and/or roving, including these to get you started:

Vertical and Horizontal Gradients

Simply layer your colors as if you were creating a color block, making sure to overlap the colors slightly. Lay your fibers lightly and burnish often for the most blended effect. Remove the batt and Z-strip and attenuate (figures 4.99 to 4.102) or diz (figures 4.103, 4.104, and 4.105) it into one long blended gradient, or diz it right off the board from your preferred direction. Don't forget about roll-ups, too, which can make easy work out of hand-pulling a special roving.

Figures 4.99, 4.100, 4.101, and 4.102 Z-strip and attenuate your batt into one long blended gradient.

Figures 4.103, 4.104, and 4.105 You may also diz your gradient right off the board.

Individually Carded Gradients

Just as in chapter 3, take two (or more) individual hues and combine them in increasing percentages, working backward from the weight of each batt and the total amount of fiber you're seeking to blend. This is a terrific way to reimagine leftover fiber scraps and/or bits of color, and work them into completely different results. You then have any number of ways to work with each individual batt in your gradient.

Figures 4.106, 4.107, 4.108, 4.109 I combined hand-dyed fine and superfine fleece (bright yellow) and longish-stapled dyed top (blue) in incremental percentages to obtain this lovely green-blue dizzed roving gradient. I blended each individual narrow batt twice before carding a third time and then diz-zing each blended color from the board vertically for a more aligned, more worsted-like, result. Each individual batt weighs exactly 0.05 ounces.

Scraptastic Sandwich Batts

Step 1: Create a layered batt using scraps of your favorite (or least favorite—you won't recognize them after this technique) fibers, colors, and/or mix-ins. Each element should be its own layer, so manage the size and width of your batty strips accordingly. I made two batts concurrently using two different blending boards, after first weighing my ingredients into two equal piles.

The base layer of each is forest green/brown, topped by a gradient of lighter colors and garneted silks.

Then I made two more batts with bolder striping repeats and stacked the layers.

Step 2: Remove each batt layer from the card cloth, whole. Stack the batts in sandwich-layer order, letting them rest until they've fully expanded. Spin your matching batts as you wish or break them down for further processing. You can even strip and recard the batts one more time—making sure to turn the insides of your strips to the outside for a softer effect.

Bottom layers

Fractals

I find fractals are a bit more straightforward when working with batts than roll-ups, as batts are more easily stripped down into smaller self-repeats than whole roll-ups are. Just as in chapter 3, these effects are more a fractal theme than a true diminishing mathematical self-repeat, but still a new way to play with fiber prep and color. See figures 4.110, 4.111, and 4.112. The initial pattern is a single repeat of berry and green (left side of the blending board) and its smaller self-repeat is next to it on the right side. I can split the batt and remove both plies, then repeat the process with as many additional ounces of fiber as needed for my spin. They may not be exact to mathematical scale, but potential diminishing-sized self-repeats and carded combinations are as vast as your imagination. If you're feeling especially daring, try one of my favorite combinations: a batt and smaller-repeating roll-ups as shown in figures 4.113, 4.114, 4.115, and 4.116.

Figures 4.110, 4.111, and 4.112 Here you see a single repeat of berry and green (left side of the blending board) and its smaller self-repeat next to it on the right side. I can split the batt and remove both plies.

Figures 4.113, 4.114, 4.115, and 4.116 Pairing wide-striped batts with narrow-striped roll-ups is another fun fractal riff.

Fancy Farm Batt

Often, the less we know, the more fearless we are in our experiments, and the better the results. Such was the case with one of my earliest batt-making efforts, when I created the most glorious batt from a gifted batch of prize-winning Corriedale locks and some commercial nylon top, both dyed by me, in sunset colors. I've never forgotten that batt, which I carded on my original 48-point, super-coarse blending board. It was eye-catching, sure, but I now understand that I was as attracted to this batt's structural blend of wavy long locks enmeshed with the shiny silken strands even more than its color complexity. Since I don't have a photo of that exact batt to include here, I've re-created it in a different color scheme, in the hopes of enticing others into working with the supplies they have on hand. The ingredients used include undyed Corriedale fleece in ecru and chocolate black, dyed Corriedale fleece, dyed nylon top, dyed firestar, and banana silk threads. Note how I comb some of the longer individual locks open against the teeth of the carding cloth to add that much more structural variation within its layers (figures 4.119, 4.120, and 4.121).

Figures 4.117 and 4.118 The top and bottom sides of my farm batt.

Figures 4.119, 4.120, 4.121 I comb some of the longer individual locks open against the teeth of the carding cloth to add more structural variation within the layers.

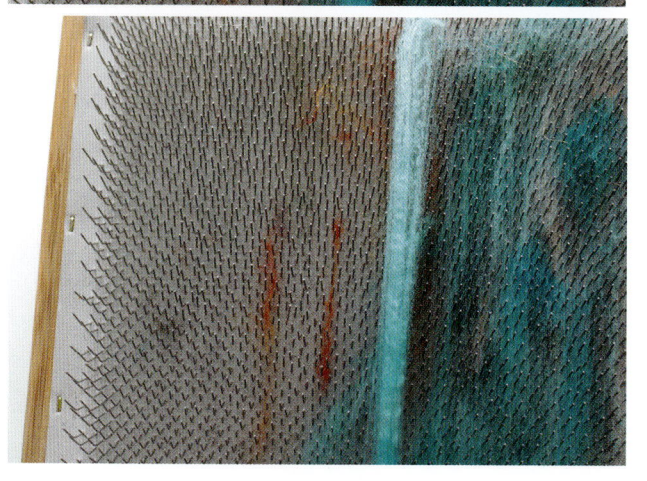

Bizzed Datty Bumps

Looking back at myself as a new spinner, I can now recognize that tactile stimulation is what called me to the craft. I had been going through a difficult time in my life and a friend kept urging me to try spinning, but I wasn't interested . . . until this same friend and I came upon a colorfully dyed, soft batt at a yarn and fiber festival. I ran over to the vendor and asked to touch the fiber and the spindle she had with it, and I've been spinning since shortly after that day. Wool breeds and their characteristics, potential ply structures, and finishing options have enchanted me ever since.

What's a bizzed datty bump? It's a batt made from gorgeous, fine fleece and luxurious silks that's then dizzed into a roving, only with the first letters of the words "batt" and "dizzed" swapped out for fun. Sometimes I use an undyed fleece, such as this chocolate-black superfine Merino, which was stellar on its own, but I blended it with beachy-colored mulberry and tussah silks and Angelina (figures 4.122 to 4.127).

Figures 4.122, 4.123, 4.124, 4.125, 4.126, and 4.127 This bizzed datty bump is made of chocolate-black superfine Merino, mulberry and tussah silks, and Angelina.

5

UNEXPECTED WAYS TO USE YOUR BLENDING BOARD

The more time you spend working with your blending board, the better able you will be to appreciate its endless options for preparing fiber and the more new ideas you'll have on how to put it to further use in your spinning journey. Here are some of my "unexpected" favorites.

BRING A BRAID OF FIBER BACK TO LIFE

Not only can the blending board be used to card a stale braid of fiber back to life, but it can also be used to rearrange color order, remove a color entirely, add a textural component to the fiber and end yarn, and more. Roll your reinvigorated fiber up into rolags, punis, etc., blend it into a batt, make a roving, or create a combination of preparations.

FLICK-CARD LOCKS AND LINE THEM UP FOR SPINNING

Your blending board may be used similarly to hand cards and flickers to flick, or tap, locks open, for a preparation that falls more on the worsted side of the woolen to worsted continuum than the woolen side. You can then line up your newly opened locks in your desired spinning order.

You're not looking to rake the fibers through the tines; you merely want the teeth to tap the end(s) of your lock open. *Be wary of getting your fingertips in the way.*

Step 1: Take a single lock and hold it securely around its middle. (If the lock is long enough, twisting it at its middle first can be helpful in securing the strands.)

Step 2: Approach the blending board from its side or bottom and lay your lock down, without dragging it against the wire.

Step 3: Take a blending brush and gently tap it against the tips of the lock, until the individual strands open. (This should work from multiple directions.)

Step 4: Turn the lock around and repeat these steps with the other end of the lock.

Step 5: Move your flick-carded lock over to the other side of the board and lay it down there, building a lineup of tapped open locks in the order in which you'd like to spin them. Continue until you've filled the length of the board.

This technique is useful for both art yarns, where you only want to open the butt end of the locks for a lock- or tailspun yarn, and for spinning a more traditional yarn that falls along the woolen to worsted continuum. Both hands will be freed up for a longer run of spinning, without interruption.

Flick-carded locks, ready to be lined up in spinning order.

FLICK-COMB YOUR LOCKS

This is another "in-between" prep, but it's more worsted in characteristics than flick-carding. Use the blending board just as you would a single hand carder or flicker brush, to comb individual locks or lock bundles open against the wire tines (figure 5.1).

Figure 5.1 Comb individual locks open against the wire tines of the blending board.

Step 1: Take your lock and twist it at the middle, then hold it securely in one hand at the twist.

Step 2: Rake the top end of the lock through the tines of your card cloth.

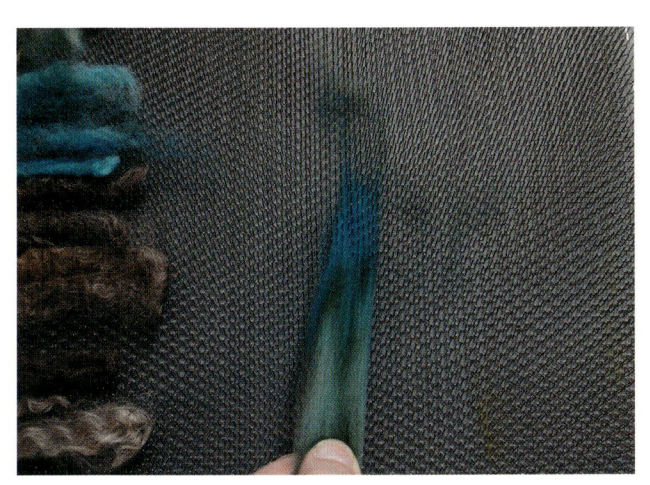

Step 3: Turn the lock around and repeat step 2.

Step 4: Line up your locks so they're ready to grab one after the next, as you spin.

DIZ A REPEATABLE "COMBED" TOP

No hackle? No problem. You can diz a repeatable, blended combed top using the bottom quarter to one-third of your blending board, and no one will be the wiser.

Step 1: Weigh out 0.20–0.25-ounce portions of your fiber. (Shown in the steps that follow: hand-dyed commercial BFL top.)

Step 2: Layer your fiber onto the bottom quarter to third of your blending board using the standard best practices (chapter 2).

Step 3: Working from one side of the overhang to the other, pull firmly on the fiber, section by section, in a downward motion. This helps to settle the fibers down into the card cloth, engaging the combing action of the wire tines for the next step.

Step 4: Starting in one corner and working horizontally across the board, diz the fiber into a sliver, making sure to utilize the tines in a combing-like fashion *by keeping your diz level with, or below, the teeth as you work.* The process is super quick, making it easy to create as much of your one-of-a-kind blend as you'd like.

WET FELTING

Wet felting is the process of taking wool fibers from their usual formation to a light and pliable fabric with the aid of soap and water (alternating hot and cold) and manual agitation of the fibers themselves. For the process to work effectively, the soapy water needs to penetrate all the way through each strand of fiber. This, combined with the manual agitation, helps to shock-shrink the strands from the inside out so the resulting fabric is much thinner than it was in its original configuration. Prior to the soapy, wet process, light staple lengths of wool are carefully laid out in even, directional layers, so that once hot and cold soapy water and agitation are added, the layers will shrink together from all directions, making for a thinner, completely stable, felted result.

A blending board isn't a necessity for wet felting, as some artists pull and arrange their staple length layers by hand, but it sure makes the process smoother . . . literally.

You can use any non-superwash-treated wool in wet felting, and embellishments like ribbon, thread, silks, bamboo, nylon and other shinies, and more, will shrink differentially and adhere to the exterior sides of your felted piece. *The wool is the inner glue of your ingredients list and goes in the middle layers of your batts.*

Here's an example. I used firestar/nylon and tussah silk on the bottom and top layers of my batt(s) (figure 5.2). The dyed purple milled BFL and Rambouillet layers went in the middle, serving as the "glue" that holds the cloth together throughout the felting and fulling process.

After applying my first shiny fibers, I then applied six light layers of my wool, alternating staple direction for each layer (vertical, horizontal, and diagonal, then working backward: diagonal (from the other direction), horizontal, and vertical for the last three (figures 5.3 and 5.4). I finished up with another round of shiny/silken fibers

Figure 5.2 The bottom layer of firestar/nylon and silk fibers goes on first.

Figures 5.3 and 5.4 Wool layers are applied in the middle in various directions.

(figure 5.5), then I pulled the batt off the blending board (figure 5.6). I made a total of four batts and used two here.

Figure 5.5 The top layer is the same mix of shinies as the bottom.

Figure 5.6 The batt is removed from the blending board. What beautiful colors!

I tore each of the two batts in half and lightly carded the top and bottom selvages together, for a longer, scarf-like accessory. Then I got to work

on shocking the fiber structures. Mostly, I called on my own knowledge of wool's reaction to water and temperature changes to guide me and made a wet mess of my living room, but I adore these initial, experimental results (figures 5.7 and 5.8).

Figures 5.7 and 5.8 The results of my wet felting experiments!

Wet felting is basic, hands-on cause-and-effect: Wool and some of its relatives shrink and roughen externally in certain conditions. It's not complicated, but felting (in general) tends to be a workout. Using a blending board saved me time and energy and made the process easier.

6

CARE AND STORAGE
OF YOUR BLENDING BOARD

KEEP IT CLEAN

Your blending board base and keel are made of hardy wood that's unlikely to warp in most environments, especially if the wood is finished. The only ongoing care it should need is periodic dusting of the wood, though you do want to keep the carding cloth clean of dust and debris. If you're making your own blending board, add your wood oil or finishing wax prior to stapling the card cloth to it and make sure it's had plenty of time to cure. You don't want any kind of oil seeping into the layers of your cloth backing.

Always use clean fibers and scoured, non-greasy fleece and locks with your blending board. Lanolin will not only coat your tines and invite rust, but it also attracts dirt and dust to the cloth itself and continues to build up. If, like me, you adore putting fleece on your board, bear in mind that dust particles *will* settle along the foundation of the card cloth—even if you don't see it happening initially. This is easily removed with the help of a small hand-held broom or a vacuum hose and brush attachment. When using a handheld duster, sweep it *upward* to dislodge and remove the dust buildup.

Figure 6.1 If you don't have a "real" cleaning brush such as the one from Brother Drum Carder (center), you still have options. The soft-bristled, hand-held duster (top) works beautifully to gently remove dust and stray fibers from my card cloth. I brush it upward against the teeth several times, starting from the bottom of the cloth and working my way up to the top. The long handle makes for quick, comfortable work. While the nylon scrubber at the bottom of the photo has stiffer bristles, it is another good cleaner. The densely packed, soft and flexible nylon bristles go deep and capture even the finest particles of dust. (I purchased these brushes from a big-box dollar-type store, but I've also seen them at many grocery stores.) Feather quills (right) are gentle for safely removing stubborn strands of fiber.

Figure 6.2 The Ashford blending brush (top) doesn't just card fibers beautifully; it also works to safely remove fiber from the carding cloth, thanks to its knee direction and fine, lightweight wire tines. I just use it held in the opposite direction when I want to clean a few stray strands from my blending board. Similarly, flexible blending brushes will do the same job when used upside down. Avoid using brushes with rigid, sharp tines. A cleaning-specific brush has lightweight, kneed tines that gently clean the fibers from your carding cloth without having to turn it around first. Just use it as you would any other brush and it will pull most of your remaining fibers from the cloth/board.

Always clean your card cloth before storage by removing leftover bits of fiber and other debris from your last carding session. Moths and other such pests are attracted to wool, so why create a potential problem for yourself when cleaning the cloth is so much easier? My favorite cleaning tools are my cleaning brush and my long-handled household dusting brush, but most any fine-tooth and light-gauge wire-tine carding brush should work, so long as you take a moment to figure out its directionality (if any) to make sure you're lifting the debris instead of further embedding it. Don't use a brush with tines that are too rigid, as this can damage your card cloth. Use light motions to avoid damaging or bending the teeth. Stubborn strands may be removed by gently using a fine, flexible knitting needle or crochet hook, the tip of a bamboo skewer, or a porcupine or feather quill—the latter being the lightest and safest for the cloth backing.

Your tines are unlikely to bend or loosen with normal and appropriate usage, though *packing the cloth too densely and pulling against them in your roll-offs can shorten their lifespan, as can working with tangled and unteased locks and too-harsh brushes.* Fortunately, replacement card or blending cloth is relatively inexpensive. (See appendix A for instructions on stapling your card cloth to your wood surface.)

To fix a bent tine or tines, take the lead out of a mechanical pencil, place the hollow pencil tip over the tine, and use the pencil as a guide to help carefully work the pin back into its proper place.

STORAGE

Your clean, debris-free blending board is easily stored by unscrewing the keel (if applicable) and filing the pieces away together on a shelf, though the handles make hanging your board (or boards) on the wall a space-saving solution. Just be certain to use hooks that have been securely anchored into the wall, either with an appropriately weighted drywall anchor or screwed into a stud. Store the board itself flat or on its side, like a book. Of course, if you've got the room to store the unit assembled, there's no need to take it apart first.

If you're traveling with your blending board, cover the tines with heavy cardboard and/or wrap the unit in bubble wrap first to keep the tines safe from damage. Disassemble the unit prior to packing it. The pieces also travel well in a large canvas-type tote but be sure to first wrap the board in bubble wrap or heavy packing paper because its sharp teeth will poke through the canvas/bag material.

Note: Always keep sharp tools out of reach of inquisitive two- and four-legged, small creatures.

ACKNOWLEDGMENTS

There are no true new discoveries in the world of handspinning. Work with any tool or spinning principle for long enough, and you will surely come to experience its vastness of possibilities. I came upon the knowledge and techniques within these pages through years of ongoing experimentation and a bit of research.

This book is not intended as a comparison of blending-board makers. Instead, I want to show today's spinners just what can be done with the unassuming blending board, no matter its maker. Thank you to Ashford Handicrafts, Majacraft, Brother Drum Carder, and Howard Brush for supplying me with quality blending boards and/or cloth, each subtly different, for use in writing this book, and to David Bennett of Howard Brush for the interview and associated information. Particular thanks to Henry and Roy Clemes of Clemes & Clemes, for their graciousness in fact-checking historical information and general knowledge-sharing. Thanks as well to Sara Gramling and her beautiful experimental hardwood blending boards, seen on the cover and in a few pages inside the book, too. These are made by her partner, Benjamin Morgan. Special thanks to my like-minded spinning pal, UK spinner James Perry, for fact-checking these pages with such integrity and for generously supplying me with his hand-dyed fiber from his Ashenflock online storefront. (Everything purple within these pages was dyed by James, as were the neon green/greys.) Thanks to Ilga Jansons and Mike Dryfoos from Edgewood Garden Studio for providing their mixed fiber packs for use in this project, and Charan Sachar for the handmade clay diz. Jillian Moreno, you are a shining example of supporting others, and Evanita Montalvo, you are a saint. Thank you for helping this novice photographer get her bearings and fall in love with a new hobby.

Despite having plotted this book for years, it took me exactly twice as long to write it as I'd imagined, as it grew in scope. I am deeply grateful to Candi Derr and Stackpole Books for their patience and for believing in the breadth of this project.

With these words, I'm officially returning to the buzz of the world after many long months of the self-sequestered quiet needed to write and photograph this work. I hope to see you out there!

APPENDIX A: DIY BLENDING BOARD

Figure A.1 This is my first homemade blending board, and it turned out to be a favorite.

Would you believe this blending board (figure A.1) is homemade? I love how it turned out, and it has become a favorite thanks to its blending cloth. This cloth was generously donated by Howard Brush (it's the company's proprietary blending-board cloth—the same one they use on their Daisy Fiber blending boards). I bought the teak cutting board at a local discount store for $14.99. The wood is solid, weighty, lightly finished, and absolutely gorgeous. This blending board has come through more than a solid year of working on this book, and it looks as good as new.

Making your own blending board is as easy as gathering together a few items. These directions will walk you through the short, inexpensive process of making a keelless blending board. If you are handy or have a friend who is, feel free to take the extra steps needed to add a swivel knob/threaded insert and keel of your choosing.

MATERIALS

- Carding cloth of your choice (read chapter 1 for detailed information on carding and blending cloths)
- Solid wood board, 0.5–0.75 inch thickness, a bit larger in dimension than your card cloth. If you'd like to seal it or finish the wood, do so and let it dry and cure fully before affixing the cloth to it.
- Light-duty upholstery staple gun (suitable for use with JT21 staples)
- Ruler and pencil
- Hand square (optional)
- C clamps (2) or quick-release clamp to hold the board in place while in use
- Retractable razor/craft knife

While I do have a drill and local hardware store for guidance, I decided against adding a keel to my blending board. My quick-release clamp (figure A.3) holds my board perfectly steady while in use, but you could add rubber gripping to the back of your board instead.

Figure A.2 The supplies needed to create your own blending board are few: A solid wood board, your preferred carding or blending cloth (shown here: Howard Brush's proprietary blending cloth), a lightweight staple gun suitable for upholstery, a tool for checking angle or a ruler (optional), and a pencil.

Figure A.3 I love my quick-release clamp. It's well worth the few extra dollars!

COST BREAKDOWN

I already own a staple gun, but a new one like it (lightweight plastic with JT21 $\frac{3}{8}$-inch staples) is about $15, including 1,000 staples. A full-sized, 11.5 x 11.5 inch square of blending or carding cloth will range from $45 to approximately $70. I already own dowels and brushes, but those may be added inexpensively (see chapters 1 and 2 for more information). For the wood board itself, I found a pack of wood cutting boards at the dollar store for $5, but I passed on those in favor of the exquisite solid teak kitchen cutting board I found at a big box discount store for $14.99.

Note that you may also purchase full DIY blending board kits from online sellers. These contain the carding or blending cloth, a pair of dowels, and usually a single (actual) carding brush for roughly an additional $30, depending on the seller.

MATERIALS	ITEMS PURCHASED NEW
Blending or carding cloth	$45–$70
Wood board	$15
Staple gun/staples	0–$15
C-clamp/quick-release clamp	$5–$15
TOTAL COST OF THE BLENDING BOARD, WITHOUT ACCESSORIES:	**$63–$115**
Brushes and dowels	$0–$40

Figure A.4 DIY Blending Board Breakdown (not including tax).

MORE EXTREME COST-SAVING OPTIONS

1. You might be able to locate a less expensive and lower quality board, such as the $5 two-pack I found at the dollar store, so a less expensive blending board could have been built for around $50. However, I would have needed to glue the boards together for proper thickness and durability.

2. My dollar store also sells dowels and various household/beauty/grooming brushes. Yours may, too.

3. Consider using a smaller sheet of carding cloth, mill ends, or scraps. I made a second, experimental blending board using a scrap piece of 90 TPI carding cloth that I ordered from the Howard Brush online outlet store ($40) and a well-worn cutting board from my kitchen ($0). The carding surface is 9.5 x 11 inches. My total cost: $40.

Figure A.5 I put together a second, truly budget, blending board for just $40 using a mill end of 90 TPI carding cloth from the Howard Brush outlet and a worn cutting board from my kitchen. It's completely functional and cost me a third of the price of even the least expensive retail blending board on the market. The carding surface is just slightly smaller than the standard full cut.

ASSEMBLY

*N*ever use adhesives in any form to affix your card cloth to the wood surface as the wire tines can settle into the glue and their pliability will be negatively impacted. Wood is the ideal base material for your blending board. It expands and contracts along with environmental changes, so it takes upholstery staples perfectly (JT21 in ⁵/₁₆- or ³/₈-inch lengths), allowing for years of happy, stable carding without a drop of adhesive.

Step 1: Make sure that the teeth of your actual carding surface fit onto your board, including indexing (the outer area of the foundation cloth where the tines have been removed to make room for stapling the cloth). If the card cloth is too long or wide for your surface, or it extends too far and there's not enough room to staple the cloth, you'll need to remove a row or two of tines yourself. Indexing is easy to create: Turn the cloth upside down on a hard work surface. Use an appropriately sized screwdriver or similar blunt implement to gently pop out the teeth in evenly spaced rows. Carefully remove any excess indexing with a razor knife. (I used a ruler and a pencil to help mark out an initial straight line to follow.) *Be sure to protect your table or work surface with heavy cardboard before cutting.*

Step 2: Align the cloth with the board using a hand square or ruler, making sure to use the points of the wire teeth as your guide and not the cut edge of the backing cloth—it may have been cut unevenly at the mill or by your own well-intended hands.

Step 3: Staple the card cloth to the board, making sure the points face upward, and the knees face downward. Once completed, you should notice how well the wire tines flex along with their foundation cloth during carding/burnishing.

APPENDIX B: COMPARISON OF BLENDING BOARDS USED IN THIS BOOK

Writing this book was never intended as a means of reviewing blending boards but instead as a way to encourage the reader to utilize the blending board they have and can afford to its fullest capabilities in their spinning and fiber preparation. That said, I'm incredibly grateful to Ashford Handicrafts–New Zealand, Majacraft, Howard Brush, and Brother Drum Carder for providing me with the range of blending boards and/or card and blending cloth to test and photograph my theories and present them here. I met Sara Gramling and her partner Benjamin Morgan at a fiber festival while well into writing and photographing this book. The two kindly loaned me three of their blending boards for added photography and for testing, and I'm so thankful.

Did I end the process with a favorite? I can say that I went into this with my own biases about TPI and my anticipated preferences and came away realizing that any make of blending board is adaptable to my needs (though admittedly, the materials and workmanship of the Ashford and Majacraft boards—which are very different boards—were standouts, as was the blending cloth used with my DIY board). This is no snub to other blending board makers, whose boards I may not have used.

The following blending boards were used in the making of this book, along with two DIY blending boards using different cloths from Howard Brush, one traditional and one blending cloth, and assembled by me:

MAKER/BRAND	SPECIFICATIONS	PRICE	COMES WITH BLENDING/ CARDING BRUSH?	NOTABLES
Ashford Handicrafts Ltd	Fine, 108-point cloth with 12 x 12 in. carding area; 3-position adjustable keel; dowels; wood and wood accessories are lightly finished/lacquered	+/- $209–$225	72-point lightly rounded blending brush and 2 dowels	Beautifully made and finished, sturdy, with an excellent carding brush.
Brother Drum Carder–Deluxe	Oak plywood with glossy polyurethane finish on all wood; 12 x 12 in., 72-point carding surface; 2 dowels	$225 ($175 for the unfinished version)	Comes with 2 plastic-handled flicker brushes with pop-out reversible card cloth (for cleaning and burnishing)	Well-constructed and finished; sturdy; tines are sharp enough to cut skin, so use with caution. Original, red-handled blending brushes were made with a more flexible tined cloth; the newer, black-handled brushes are just as lightweight and comfortable to use, but the teeth are notably more rigid and may damage your card cloth. Made in the USA.
Galaxy Fibers	72 TPI card cloth with 11 x 11.5 in. carding surface; made of hardwoods and/or exotic woods; 2-position matching keel; comes with 2 thick dowels and a true blending brush; all wood is fully sanded and finished	n/a	Comes with a true blending brush and 2 thick dowels	Crafted from premium wood with attention to craftsmanship and finishing details; handmade in the USA; makers are unlikely to continue in this particular field.
Heavenly Handspinning (no longer in production)	TPI coarse cloth with 12 x 12 in. working surface; 5-position adjustable keel; double handle	n/a	No—came with moderately stiff-bristled household paintbrush	I love everything about the design, sturdiness, and usability of this blending board, though it's the heaviest of them all. The coarse card cloth makes for remarkably airy results. The upper and lower belly grooves and vertical thumb/finger grips are genius.

Continued on next page

MAKER/BRAND	SPECIFICATIONS	PRICE	COMES WITH BLENDING/CARDING BRUSH?	NOTABLES
Majacraft	72 TPI card cloth with 8.3 x 11.8 in. carding surface; 2-position keel; thick, non-slip foam backing and foam finishing area on front bottom of the board	$235–$275	No—came with a household paintbrush for smoothing and tamping	There's something about the narrower size, well-constructed pieces and beautiful finishing, and the sturdy curved metal handle that makes this blending board perfect for moving around the house and/or taking to workshops—just add a couple suitable carding brushes for optimal results. It's sturdy and does a terrific job with every technique. The smaller size also makes quick work of making larger-sized single rolags efficiently and scalably. Excellent carding cloth.
DIY blending board No. 1 (see appendix A)	Proprietary Howard Drum blending cloth with 12 x 12 in. carding surface. TPI is "approximately 72."	(Blending-board cloth donated by Howard Drum) plus $15 teak cutting board	n/a	I absolutely love this cloth and my finished board.
DIY blending board No. 2	90 TPI carding cloth sold as a "second"	$45 plus my own free, well-worn, wood cutting board	n/a	This may not be as attractive as my other blending boards, but I'm so pleased with its usability and its affordability.

RESOURCES AND CREDITS

Amos, Alden. *The Alden Amos Big Book of Handspinning.* Interweave Press, 2001.
Fannin, Allen. *Handspinning: Art and Technique.* Van Nostrand Reinhold, 1970.
Field, Anne. *Spinning Wool: Beyond the Basics.* Shoal Bay Press Ltd., 1995.
Larson, Kate. *The Practical Spinner's Guide: Wool.* F+W Media, 2015.
Menz, Deb. *Colorworks: The Crafter's Guide to Color.* Interweave Press, 2004.

Ashford Handicrafts/Ashford Wheels and Looms—Ashford.co.nz
Majacraft—Majacraft.co.nz
Brother Drum Carder—brotherdrumcarder.com
Howard Brush—howardbrush.com

Ashenflock—www.etsy.com/shop/Ashenflock
CF Merchantile—www.etsy.com/shop/CFMerchantile
Creative with Clay—creativewithclay.com
Edgewood Fiber Arts—https://edgewoodgardenstudio.com/
Gregory Pencheff Woodturning—GVPencheff.Etsy.Com
PLY Magazine—Issue 37; Summer 2022
Spin Off—Spring 2016
My own massive fiber stash!

GLOSSARY

Blending cloth—A carding cloth that's been adapted specifically for use on a blending board. It may have slightly longer tines and blunter tips for safety, plus other traits.

Burnishing brush—A specialty brush used in carding to pack as much fiber as possible into the card cloth and around the cloth's set-in tines.

Card cloth—The flexible cloth with set-in wire tines used in carding equipment including hand cards, drum carders, and blending boards.

Combed top—Fiber prepared by hand-combing staple lengths that are all facing the same direction, butt to tip, so they're parallel and all short bits are removed. For a true, 100 percent combed top, finish with a diz.

Commercial top—Fiber that's combed and aligned mechanically with mill equipment. This is the majority of the fiber that's sold online and often (mis-)labeled as "roving."

Double carding—Carding a batt a second time.

Flick-carding—Using a hand card or flicker brush to tap open the ends of a lock of wool.

Flick-combing—Dragging a lock of wool through the tines of a flick brush or hand card.

Fractal spinning—Based on the mathematical theory of complex wholes. This is a style of color management in spinning, not an actual spinning method. Applied to handspinning, a whole repeatable color pattern is split into smaller repeats. The original pattern is spun as 1 ply and the smaller splits are spun as the second (and third, if further self-repeats are broken down even smaller).

Garneting—Reusing textile waste by turning it back into a fibrous, spinnable form and blending with spinning fiber.

Hue—Term used for a color family, such as greens, reds, etc.

Indexing—Removal of the U-shaped wire tines along the outer strip of a carding cloth, leaving the cloth's foundation for use in stapling to its intended surface.

Marl—Two or more colors spun together but still remaining distinctive.

Mix-ins/add-ins—Term I use for the fun bits of color, texture, threads, and so forth, that I like to card into my fibers.

Roving—Continuous fiber that's been carded and is mostly parallel but still contains different lengths jumbled within. It has a slight hint of natural twist to it.

Shade—Darkening/deepening a color with the addition of black.

Sliver—Continuous length of parallel and uniform fiber with no natural twist.

Space-dyed yarn—Hand-dyed yarn with incrementally appearing color repeats.

Tint—Lightening a color with the addition of white.

Tone—Adding gray to a color or hue.

TPI and PPI—Tines/teeth per square inch and points per inch on a carding cloth. Both measure the same.

Variegated yarn—Yarn that's been space dyed with incremental color repeats.

VM—Short for "vegetable matter," or the bits of hay, grass, and other debris sometimes left in farm wools after processing. A little bit of VM left in a farm-raised, uncoated sheep's wool is normal and should be easy to pick out in spinning.

Wire fillet—Card cloth in a continuous roll.

Wire sheet—Card cloth made in sized sheets.

INDEX